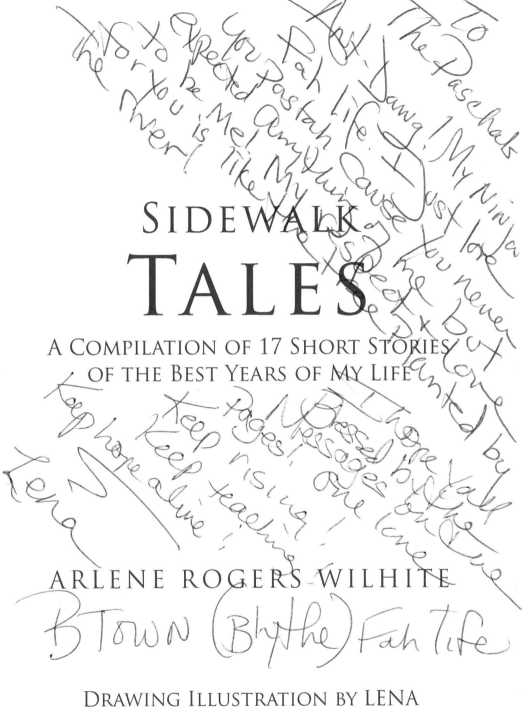

SIDEWALK
TALES

A COMPILATION OF 17 SHORT STORIES
OF THE BEST YEARS OF MY LIFE

ARLENE ROGERS WILHITE

DRAWING ILLUSTRATION BY LENA
MODELED BY REGINAE D. THORNHILL

PAGE PUBLISHING, INC.
Conneaut Lake, PA

First originally published by Page Publishing 2020

ISBN 978-1-68456-010-3 (pbk)
ISBN 978-1-68456-011-0 (digital)

Printed in the United States of America

To my favorite girl, Ms. Hardy, Precious Hardy Barnett, you inspired me to set my goals as high as you were tall to me so long ago at San Pedro Elementary School. Your gesture of love, giving Angela Stone and reflect on me those necklaces, touched my life forever. You showed the kind of unconditional love Jesus teaches us to have. As bad as I was, you took the time to show me I was worth caring for.

I dedicate this book and all the educational goals that I have achieved to you and Mr. Kusomoto, who taught me to appreciate art, and it helped me calm the beast inside of me.

Sincerely, Arlene Rogers
Associate in Arts liberal Studies
Associate in Arts Human Services
Bachelor of Arts, Studio Art
Master of Business Administration
Doctoral Candidate Social Behavior and
Community Services Leadership

Sweet Pea, I cannot remember the exact year we met, but we had so much fun that one night up in the Dunes Motel, and I said when I write my book I was going to dedicate it to you. My only regret is I never learned your first or last name. All I know is Sweet Pea from Sacramento. I hope one day someone reads this, or you yourself and you contact me and let me know you are okay. I can only pray. That would be a joy to my heart as you gave me joy that night clowning around up in that room.

Dedications

I dedicate this book to the Rose Brothers, Soul Brothers 77 (I am inclined to believe that that slab of stone had been there since 1977, since it was written and circled like that). They may be gone now, but I will remember them forever and reflect on how they changed my life with a simple action of engraving their names in stone (the cement had probably just been laid). It intrigues me that I feel as though that encounter was meant to be and just for me, and we only met passing on a sidewalk.

To Alvin Jacocks, A love like a ship lost at sea; love always.

I would like to thank my husband Stephen who encouraged me to not give up my dream to write my book, and Renee Goodwin at Country Village sitting in computer room night after night sorting papers with me, and below are pictures of the sidewalk that inspired me to write my stories. The originals were destroyed in a fire, but had it not been for this sidewalk, my tales probably have never been told.

Contents

Prologue

I left my house in a hurry. I was out of *medicine* and was heading to downtown San Bernardino to find a *doctor* to help me. *I was looking for the dope man.* I decided to go the route on Third Street by the San Bernardino Metro Link Train Station. I walked across the street from there because I didn't want to change my pace crossing the street, so I started on the side nearest the little mall to my right. It was a two-way street, and I was on the right side moving eastward.

I had walked that street many times through rain and heat, days and nights. I made it to my *doctor's appointment* and practically ran back. I walked so fast trying to get home to administer my dosage, (tongue in cheek). I came back the same way I had gone, on the same sidewalk; and just as I got to the first palm tree, when I had gone downtown, was now the first palm tree as I headed westward, which was the last palm tree going, I stubbed my toe and cursed.

I looked to see what I had stumped my toe on, and there was a little rock on the pavement of the sidewalk. How I missed it on the trip going. I don't know. As I bent to pick it up, as though I was going to have a boxing match with it for being in my path, I noticed a list of names engraved in the cement's square. I forgot about the rock and the potential *boxing match*, and the pain I was feeling in my toe and kicked at the gravel that must have been the family of the rock that attacked me, and brushed the gravel away from the engravings. Something made me stop to read the names.

There were several names printed on the slab, (I hope I remembered them all): *Michael Rose, Dwayne rose, Wayne Rose and Anderson Rose Jr., Robert Rose, Roderick Rose and Hubert Rose, Andrew Rose with Soul Brothers 77* (circled). The last part, 77, I noticed that after another trip. I was suddenly enticed by this slab of cement of names, and I stood there wondering, *How I could have passed this way so many times and never noticed all these names before? Who were they? Why did they write their names there? Who wrote their names there? What were they doing before they stopped to write their names? Did one person write all the names? Were they Black? White? Mexican? What?* I was too curious. If I had been a cat, I would be dead today. Now this really flooded my curiousity to know, *were they gangbangers? Why did it even matter so fiercely?* Suddenly, I just had an urge to know *who were these men.* All these thoughts shot through my mind as I decided almost aloud. *Let me get home to my room so I can get my look on* (that's another way to say *get high*), and I had everything I needed to get high too. All the beer I needed and paraphernalia. The only thing that was missing was what I held in my hand.

I was on *a mission* but still intrigued by the Roses. I really wanted to get to the bottom of the names inscribed on the ground. The aching of my big toe was gone. My flip flops were clacking under my feet hard. I let my fingers play in the holes of the fence that separated the sidewalk from the buildings along the walk. I started thinking, *Man, if sidewalks could talk, what tales could they tell?* Then I thought, *Most of all my adventures, challenges, and events that happen in life happened on sidewalks of some kind.*

I wondered about writing about my life and narrowing it down by stories that happened on sidewalks. As I walked along that day, I thought, *What could I call it? Sidewalk Stories? Nah, I surmised, too flat. Tales of Sidewalk Stories?* Nope, boring! Then it came to me *Sidewalk Tales? Yeah, that has a Stephen King ring to it. I loved it! It wouldn't be about horror or mayhem, or would it be? Yeah, I've done some pretty horrific things that could cause some mayhem!* Hence, *Sidewalk Tales* was born. From that day forward, I walked by that square of names, assuring myself I didn't *imagine* it all; and I became more in tuned to the *message* I felt those names sent me.

The message I heard was, "Write your book, girl. Write about your life and connect it to the Rose brothers. Talk about how roses have always been your favorite flower, about how painting a rose was your breakthrough to painting more, and how you found out the names on that slab of cement were once a part of your family!" Yeah, come to find out two of my daughters, Audrey and Rhonda, knew the Roses, Michael and Duane. And my son Bobby knew them all. And after asking around, I found out that they were black (most of them, if not all are deceased); and yes, that's why soul Brothers 77 was in the lower right-hand corner of the cement. *They were truly soul brothers*. I didn't notice the soul brothers 77 until I came back to take pictures of the slab, and I poured water on it to clean it.

Unfortunately, the pictures of the names were burned in a fire where I had my things in storage. I wanted the pictures so badly for this book, but I went back and took pictures of where they once were. Apparently, when they remodeled the mini mall by the train station, they reconstructed everything, even the sidewalks around the perimeter—whether they needed to be repaired or not. The ground was dug up right where that slab of cement was. I was devastated. I almost felt as though it was a deliberate attack against me. That was history uprooted—black history to me—once I realized who they were. My intentions were to find their family and show them the legacy they left on the streets of San Bernardino. I would love to tell them how that inspired me to write this book. This book I had promised my friends long ago I would write but never did. I found a niece of the Rose family on Facebook and was able to tell her what I was writing and about the names on the cement; and as I imagined, she was excited about it until I told her the bad news, that it was destroyed, but at least I found a family member to share my plight with.

It is funny how I was going downtown to buy a rock to smoke, lead me on the path to a rock that penetrated my flip flops to a slab of rock that penetrated my heart. I would have never imagined I would get inspiration by a stubbed toe and seven names written in stone literally.

Wall Street

L iving on Wall Street was like living on one of those streets you see in the opening of a Spike Lee film: kids running around the neighborhood, folks on the porch playing dominoes, and talking big trash to one another. There weren't too many sirens blaring in those days, at least not in comparison to if you go into the city these days. You can hear sirens on and off of the freeways in the hoods all day.

All of the most important years of my life, were spent on that street. I met all the friends I would keep forever and fell in love numerous times, (with school-girl crushes), toward every boy I would later see again and still love. Now that I am an adult, I can almost think that maybe it is where God wanted me to be. Even despite all the negative things that happened to me later on, I still think, God was with me all the while.

At 2325 ½, Wall Street was a magical place to me. It was a magical place of laughter and pain both, and sad times. It was a four-plex structure and the *Metropolis of porch living!* Everyone sat on our porch: kids, babies, child molesters, gangsters, mail carriers, milkmen, teenagers, insurance agents, senior citizens, gay-men, gay-women, police officers, and vagabonds; and I was in the midst of it all. It was like living in a circus that never travelled but always had enough performers to entertain.

My dad moved us to Los Angeles after he had left our hometown, Blythe California, a small desert town east of Los Angeles. Apparently, he had a run in with the law, and some people and just felt it best for his life that he leave that little town or come up dead. I heard bits and pieces of the story as I grew up and found out later it was over one of his best friend's death all this transpired. After he sent for us, he lived in one place; and we lived with my cousin, June-June and his wife, Lapores. All the kids called her Aunt Lay-Lay. She was my cousin Dottie's mom. It was a big pink two–story house on the corner of Twenty-Third and Wall Street. It would be my first place of resident on Wall Street but not my last. Before I turned fourteen years old, we had moved to our own place across the street from the big pink house I called it, to some courts and then to the four-plex across the streets from the courts. So basically, we zig-zagged from house to house on Wall Street but never moved *off* the street.

My first *home* was 2315 South Wall St. By this time, I was old enough to go to school and had to learn where I lived. I was four when we left Blythe. I was small, but I remember everything that has ever happened to me. Sometimes I think that is why I am sup-posed to be writing this book. While we were living with my cousins, there were three other families that lived in that big house. It was a four-plex as well, two apartments upstairs, and two downstairs. We lived in one of the upstairs one. The other families that lived there were the Smiths; and Mrs. Florence and her children—Calvin, Ruby and Gloria—they all became a big part of my life. Mrs. Smith was the reason I ended up going to Sister Casoli church, but that's another story. Her son, Jackie (who was later killed as a teen), was good friends with my brother, Charlie; and we all went to church together. Ruby and Gloria became my big sisters; and to this day, we still are in contact with one another.

We were all intertwined in one another's lives; and before Dottie and her family moved, we all moved to the courts across the streets and watch them tear the big pink complex down that was the needle and thread that wove us all together. We lived on Wall Street until I was fourteen years old. I saw families come and go, saw people beaten, go to jail, wives catch their husbands cheating, and vice versa. Families helping families and kids fighting then making up and play-ing as though anything never happened, and yet we stayed. I later heard parents of my friends say they couldn't go on Wall Street, only to find out the reason was because they hung on the street them-selves. For some reason, people seem to gravitate to Wall Street; and

I believed it was the best street in Los Angeles to live. Wall Street was my world.

One day, we woke up; and the city had decided to build a park in the big empty field on our street that was half of a block long. The empty field was a third of the block on Wall Street, Twenty-Fifth Street; and Trinity St. like a box with only three sides, and they opted to name it Trinity Park. Once that park was built, it was as though New Jerusalem itself had come down through the skies. We, the kids, couldn't wait for them to finish. We played on the empty lot anyway, so we continued to do so even when the heavy operating equipment began rolling in to move the debris. That just made it the more exciting! Especially when we would catch couples kissing and *necking* in the parked cars and scare them as we banged on the cars.

The Ramirez Family lived on the street for as long as we did; and for years after we'd left, they were still on the block. Mercedes, who was my childhood friend, eventually moved in the last house we lived in on Wall Street in the big white four-plex. We moved into after we left the courts. In fact, it was her grandfather (abuelito) who taught me how to speak Spanish. Mercedes, her brothers Richard and Chuy, were like my family. We ate together. I stayed at their house, watched television with them. They taught me loteria (a Mexican game like Poke-Keno or Bingo) and to do the cumbia (a Mexican cha-cha-like dance). Their eldest sister, Yolie, whose name was Yolanda, taught us that. She also taught me to sing *Angel Baby* by Rosie and the Originals. She was in love with a guy name Angel too, who she later married. We were family, no color lines. And then there was Cuca (pronounced koo-ka), she played football (soccer) like a female Pele'. She lived in Mexico and would only visit, but she was so sweet and couldn't speak a lick of English but was always smiling and playful. They taught me what love is from others beside my family, and I will always be grateful for them. I can truthfully say that everything I learned in life, I learned from living on Wall Street.

When I go back to Wall Street, the street looks smaller than it did when I was a kid. The buildings are colorful, and trees planted in yards where only grass used to be. I think of all the stories I could tell, of all the people that walk the sidewalks. I have so many memories and remember all the faces that passed that way. I remember those who touched our lives and whose lives we touched. My mother fed so many people, nursed so many people back to health, and took so many people in. I guess that's why I can't help being the same way. We co-existed. It was not a question of who had what or who's was the best or least. We lived around people who had money and people who barely could eat. Sometimes, I reflect on the fact that maybe we were a little too close to one another; but nonetheless, we were all in a good place on Wall Street.

I thank God that there were no real tragedies that occurred on my street. We had fights and car accidents and people dying of illnesses and the like, but there were no drive-by and shootings and raping of that nature, although it happened *around* us. It happened, and we heard about it; but for the most part, people on Wall Street looked out for the next person. To some degree, we all suffered. For instance, as great as I want to believe Wall Street was, I was molested, and no one seemed to notice or care or if they did know they didn't come to my rescue; and I have often wondered, *why me? Why was I the spotted calf? Why did I stand out? Why am I still alive to write about it?*

My childhood was cut short on Wall Street, and I withdrew, and I became a loner to some degree. And the days of running from boys and climbing trees in the park and rolling in boxes that once had refrigerators in them, that we made into tanks, came to an abrupt halt. Just when I was beginning to experience little-girl crushes on little-ugly boys (that's what you called the ones you liked) and going to the movies and skating along the sidewalks, were becoming an everyday joy for me, I had to give it all up to save my life because no one else seemed to care that I needed a savior. That is no one but the savior Himself; and at the time, I didn't even know he was saving me.

Wall Street was magical. Did I say that? It was. We were kids who made our own bikes, skateboards before it became a fad. We made our own go-carts, real Lil' Rascals. We were businessmen and businesswomen, selling pop bottles and washing cars, going to the store for the elders. We were artists and bakers, preachers and teachers; and we all got our start on the sidewalks of Wall Street. But then somehow, we became drug addicts and survivors of abuse and thugs and killers and gangbangers; and somewhere along the way, we just became lost in societies cracks in its sidewalks. Not all of us but enough of us. We all went to church, but we didn't know God Almighty. Satan was watching us all. We were being set up for failure even before we realized we had a destiny to fulfill. Why we were never on the six o'clock news I will never know; but for the Grace of God, after all we were careless, reckless kids with one thing on our minds, *fun*.

We weren't bad. We were just kids. We ventured in every neighborhood around us as though they were ours; and each child I ever played with, always wanted to come on *your street*. "Let's go to your street," they would say. Many people came and went on Wall Street. Even though I later had my problems to deal with, it was a good street to live on. I would live there all over again if I had to because I learned character and found strength on that street. I found God on that street. It was all the home I knew. We felt loved, and I think that is what made that street so great, is that others felt that love as well. It was always a joy to come home from school or a vacation back to my street, and I still get that feeling when I go back to Los Angeles, and I can visit my old stomping grounds. I felt about Wall Street as I do about God. There should always be a path that leads to home, and I have found and discovered how all sidewalks should and do lead to Jesus if we just open our eyes and look for Him. He is there.

Sister Casoli

I was born in a Baptist household. Having Christ as my *personal savior* was just an expression that I didn't really understand but knew I had to embrace Him as my own just as everybody else did. My grandmother, mother, and my aunts went to church, sang in church, and went to clubs when they were not in church. They played cards, drank, and had fun; but come Sunday, somebody was in church! Usually the kids.

I was born in Blythe California. One day, my daddy sent for my mom, myself, and my brother, Charlie; and we all moved to Los Angeles, California, to Twenty-Third and Wall Street and lived there from the time I was four, going on five years old until I was four-teen. It seems as though I lived there all my life. I grew up fast and furious on that street; and if it had not been for Sister Jean Casoli, Lord knows what kind of life my foundation would have taken me to. Life was already challenging for me at four years old. Can you imagine me without God in my life? Somehow I knew that if I didn't have Him in my life, my life would be hell; but through the abuse days, teen pregnancy, and promiscuity, I always remembered that bell Sister Casoli would ring out of the window of her blue van, gathering children to come to church. I still can hear the ringing in the back of my head, reminding me, *'Jesus is going to ring a bell (trumpet); and He's gonna gather His children in the clouds, and He's coming to get me.'*

Sometimes I would hear her from the back room of the house. In my bedroom, I could faintly hear the bell; and I would jump out of bed and run to the door and see the blue van with the white lady going down the street. Knowing I had missed her again, I would run back into the house to ask my mom if I could walk to church. We had been knowing about Sister Casoli's church because when we met Sister Smith when we first moved out here, she introduced us all to that little church. I reminded my mom where the church was, and she said I could go, to be just be careful and come straight home. I dashed away as she was speaking. During those times, we weren't really scared of abductions and such as it is nowadays.

I was headed out the door, and my dad called me back in and asked if I had bathed, and I lied and told him I had. He went into the bathroom, and the tub was bone dry, and he told me to get back in there and take a *damn bath*, all in one breath or stay home. So I ran into the bathroom again and ran the water and took a quickie bath and redressed and was running out the door. I was excited. I wanted to be in church. I had heard about how the lady gives goodies after church; and during the holidays, she would give baskets of food and presents and take kids on trips; and the kids get Kennedy halves, and I knew that I couldn't miss all that!

As I walked down the sidewalk, I came across two girls on the other side of the street. They were going in the same direction as I was. When we made it to the corner of Twenty-Third Street and Wall, the older girl asked me if I was going to Sister Casoli's church as well; and I said I don't know her name. She rings the bell by my house.

The girl went on, "That's her. My name is Nancy, and this is my sister Anita, and what's your name?

And I said, "Arlene."

And she said, "You can walk with us," and I did. I walked with them every chance I could, and I walked right on into their lives, and they became my family. For many days and nights, I went to Sister Casoli's church. She, to this day, was the most angelic woman I'd ever seen. I believed she was black because I'd never known a white lady with *nappy* hair and rubbery skin who loved little black kids so much. She'd go out of her way to bring them to church and teach them to read, to sing, to praise God, to love Him, to really love him, and what it really meant to have Him as a personal savior.

Sister Casoli showed movies that I still can find on YouTube and taught us scriptures I still remember. She used a slide projector to make her points about who Jesus was and taught us bible verses with that machine as we held our hands and fingers up to make birds and ducks or just silly faces. It was great seeing our silhouettes on the screen. She had to love us 'cause we were rambunctious. She made learning fun depending on the bible verses a child could recite, determined the size of the prize you could receive. No one went home empty handed. She would spank us too if we got out of hand and take us to our parents. I admired her. She would sing and try to hit the highest notes. Every time I hear *He Lives*, I think of her, holding that note forever. It seemed to the point of getting on her tip toes to do it. The memory warms my heart. Some of the notes she hit. Some of them she missed, and I guess I inherited that from her because I will get in front of people and sing my heart out, on the note or off. It is all to the glory of God; and that is how she made me feel do it for the glory of God, and don't worry about how others see *you*. I sing in her spirit today.

One day, my mother gave me money for church. I had been going to Sister Casoli's church ever since I came to live on Wall Street and even more regularly as I became of age. Some friends and I arrived at church early, and sis Casoli was out getting the Smith Family (not the Smiths who lived by us). They lived in Aliso village in East Los Angeles; so we, some other kids and I, went to the local Mexican Bakery on Maple and Twenty-Second Street, and we bought candy and Mexican pun (bread), cupcakes, and sodas. We had been caught so many times by Sister Casoli that it had become a game to try to beat her back to the church before she could catch us. On this particular day that I am writing about, one of the kids ran around to the bakery to tell us that Sister Casoli had made it back to the church, and that she was looking for us. She knew our parents sent us to church faithfully. So we all ran out the store. Some stashed their goodies in bushes. Some threw their stuff away, and some ate as much as they could, and I hid mine. I was not about to throw my food away. The kid told us she had said that if we were spending *God's money*, we would be in trouble. Now that was scary to me. She

24

had never *said* that *before*, but usually I would be the one asking other kids for a soda or something, but this time, I could splurge, so I was not giving up my treats. So we all high-tailed it on back to church.

As we entered the church, it was as though a glow was around Sister Casoli's head. Granted her hair was blonde and wavy, and there was a light illuminating from the small pulpit she taught from. I would venture to say I was being convicted before I knew it. She was leaning on the altar as though she was tired, just silently watching us fall in, guilty, scared; and some of us still with the evidence around our mouths. The other kids turned around in their seats to see us all file in as well. Some snickering. Some of the adults scrawling at us, and Sister Casoli waited until we all sat down, and she looked at each of us. It was the longest look ever. My friend Ava and I tried to hide by sitting way in the back row of the pews. Sister Casoli started talking about our parents giving us money to bring to church for the Lord's offering, not for the stores and how when we spend money that's for the church. We were stealing from God. My whole body seemed to begin to shake as if I were on a treadmill with one of them belts about my waist. I couldn't stop it. My heart began to beat fast, and I felt as though I was going to explode, or was that my imagination.

Whatever it was, when she asked her next question, "Who stole from God today?" She continued, "If anyone had money for God and went to the store, stand up and come down and ask god for forgiveness."

The beating of my heart made me get up, and some of the kids laughed as I walked up to her. Me who was determined not to give my food up, with tears in my eyes, I began to empty my pockets and gave it to her; and she took my foods and turned me around to face the church. Then she said these words, "God is going to bless you for being honest and wanting forgiveness. Are you sorry?"

I cried and said, "Yes."

And she *hugged* me and said, "You may go back to your seat. You are forgiven." I was still sniffling when I heard her asked if there was anyone else who wanted to confess. She wanted to know if there was anyone else as brave as I was to stand up, and a boy stood up, and Sister Casoli had asked him if he did it because I stood up, or was he really sorry. And the young man confessed he was sorry also, and she told him to sit down, and he was forgiven as well. But before he sat down, she made sure she told him and others not to wait until someone else confesses. That they must confess on their own.

I forgot who it was. I was still in shock that she hugged me instead of punished me; and on top of that, she called me brave. I was confused in my mind; but later in my life time, I learned that when a person gives unconditional love and unconditional forgiveness, it is a true act of God. My heart was slowly starting to beat normally. I felt different. I felt as though I was going through some kind of change. I was not the same after that-still bad but very conscious of what I did and what I said. When I went back to my seat, one of the other girls sitting in front of Ava and me turned to me and asked me, "Why did you do that? That was stupid." But to this very day, I believe God is still blessing me for being honest and asking for forgiveness that day. She apparently didn't get any of what Sister Casoli said that morning because if she did she would not have asked me that *stupid* question. It reminds me of the scripture where Jesus says, "Whoever belongs to God hears what God says: the reason you do not hear is that you do not belong to God" (John 8:47, NIV).

On my way home that afternoon, as I walked along the sidewalks, I felt good inside. I felt strong for some reason, and I felt light on my feet like I was being carried home. I heard them say the truth will set you free. I didn't know that back then, but I still feel that freedom, as though it has never left me, and I am still riding on that freedom from so long ago.

Night, Night

This is a special story to me. I was going to take it out, but I had to pray over it because I didn't want to offend anyone, but I wanted to tell it because it taught me a lot throughout the years. I have held it in my heart. Some of the details are blurry, and I had to accentuate it with word fillers and such because my memory is fading; and after all, it was fifty something years ago. This is about a kidnapping that took place when we were kids. I thought it was a kidnapping, and I asked one of my cousin if she remembered the event, and she said she did and gave me her account. Needless to say, our stories differed, but one thing we did agree upon is that her little sister was being kidnapped.

I haven't seen Night in thirty something years. The last time I saw her, I believe it was at Aunt Lay Lay's funeral, and recently, when I became her friend on Facebook, and we have been in contact since. In fact, I just remembered her real name, Maxine. She was not my blood cousin. She is the cousin of my cousin Dottie, on Dottie's mother side of the family. We weren't raised that we were *friends but kinfolk*. When you start talking kinfolk, you are talking step-family, twice removed family and blended family. We were none of that, but we were raised as cousins nonetheless.

We weren't the best kids in the neighborhood but neither were we the worse. We just came from a generation of people who loved to party and who didn't mind fighting, especially if you messed with one of their own. So we mimicked what we saw and heard. Albeit we were taught not to go around picking fights nor disrespecting people, especially our elders. Talk about getting a good licking, disrespect an old person if you want too; but we were known for finishing a good fight.

This particular day, we had all been playing in the piles of dirt that was on the land across the street from my house on Wall Street in Los Angeles. It was one of those days when it seemed all the *cousins* were over, and the parents were in the house playing music and cards and cooking, just having a good time. The city had decided to build a park for the area; and daily, we would watch the trucks haul in dirt and level the land and plant trees and lay cement and tar. When I say *we*, I am talking about the kids who lived on the street and the adults who frequented our porch. My cousin Night and her family did not live on that street, but they came over regularly on the weekends or special occasions. So whenever we could, we would run over to the dirt lot and play; and the men would chase us away. We made a game out of being chased by the construction crew, played made-up games to run from one pile of dirt to the next dig tunnels, and chase boys we liked and beat up those we didn't like. And they would turn the game around and chase us and beat us up. It was a cat and mouse good time. We were kids, and we made the most of our days and nights. Sometimes we'd play until ten o'clock at night if it were the weekend and our parents were partying (and it seemed as though they always were). The big kids would watch us (then they would forget about us), and it would be 12:00 a.m. before we kids settled down.

As the evening drew on this day, we were all playing; and it was nearing dusk, but it was still light out. We all realized my cousin Night was walking at a steady pace with a girl in a long white coat (and she was white). As she was looking back at us, she wasn't saying anything. Night had to be around five or six if not younger. She wasn't crying, and we all looked around and started calling her. The girl started walking faster, and we all went chasing after the girl. The grown-ups were still partying and not knowing what was going on, and we were outside trying to stop this kidnapping. Night's oldest sister ran after that girl and chased her down with us all trailing behind her. We cut through the dirt fields, glass twigs, half of trees and glass, just screaming and yelling until we finally caught up with the girl, snatched Night from her and was about to beat her up. Night's sister Tee was asking the girl what was her problem and was she crazy, and it was chaotic! Poor Night, she still did not seem to know what was going on. So the girl, who lived around the corner, told Tee she just wanted to take her home to play with her. Well that really incited Tee's anger, and she lit into the girl all over again, telling her that she don't steal people to take them home to play with. It was scary at the time; but in hindsight, I laugh because when I asked Tee if she remembered that story, she gets all angry and excited as though it is happening all over again. But that was her little sister, so I can understand that.

We all walked back to the house, all of us in Night's ear, telling her not to be doing anything like that again. We went back to the porch and told Tee's mom what had happen; and at first, I don't think they believed us at all. It was that, or they were so intoxicated that they thought it was funny; but eventually, they listened to us because Tee is a convincing person, and she was not going to let them think that it was all a joke. Once they were convinced we were not lying, they told us to stay in the house; and we all fussed and hissed and cried that it was not dark outside. After we tired-out and all the families started preparing to go to their homes, we began playing tag for another forty-five minutes. We kids always tried to make every visit last.

I think it was my aunt Maxine who yelled, telling us all to stop playing and told Tee and them to get in the car; and we stopped playing, and they piled in their cars. I remember my cousins getting into two cars. Dottie came with her parents, and she was an only child, but I think one of her other cousins went home with them. We were all waving good-bye. I hated to see them go. I didn't have any sisters, and my brother was not trying to play with me this night, so it was a bittersweet moment, tired; but if they all got out of the car right then, I would have loved it. In the car, I saw kids crawling over little Night. She was such a pretty chocolate baby—big round eyes, smooth dark skin like a little black doll—just innocently sitting there, not knowing she was almost a victim of God knows what. None of us for that matter truly realized what could have been done to her. Who knows? Maybe that girl's parents had told her to bring her or some child back home, or she couldn't come home. I don't know. After watching *Criminal Minds*, I know now that anything is possible and could have been then as well.

I just shudder to think if we hadn't looked up and saw that girl walking off with Night what would have been. I have always loved Night and all my cousins. Night was just the baby then. She was so small; and as the car cranked up and they were pulling off, we stood on the porch, waving and shouting good byes; and I yelled it or I whispered it, "Night, Night." One thing I did realize is that she was safe. She was going home, and we saved her from the awful night on the sidewalk that could have led her to hell, but we will never know. And I thank God for that.

Big Rebecca

If I never knew I was a potential track star, I sure knew it the day Big Rebecca went after me coming from Church. As I have said so many times, Sister Casoli went everywhere gathering children for Sunday School—in the Twenties, Thirties, Forties (streets in Los Angeles)—and as far as Aliso Village and other areas. Rebecca was fortunate as I was to know about Christ Mission Bible School Church, which was pastored by Sister Jean Casoli; but to this day, just this day, I wish Rebecca had not known Sister Casoli, her church or me!

I had it bad being a show off in front of a lot of people especially if I had one in the bunch to feed on my mischievousness, and it seemed someone would always start the trouble, but I'd end up in the trouble. Whether I was going to the principal's office (getting swats), getting suspended, you name it. I just never knew when enough was enough. Everyone knew Rebecca. We all called her Big Rebecca and a whole lot more. She lived on Twenty-Second and San Pedro across from my friend Brenda Whitten.

She had two sisters, Delores and Margie and a brother Tommy respectively. He used to get teased as well because he was blinded in one eye; but kids can be so cruel, they don't care about defects like that, not in a caring way. They don't, but they care to make fun of another person's defect, as we did and regretted, messing with Big Rebecca. My brother went to school with Tommy and his sisters, but my brother didn't do childish things as I did, talking about people and messing around like that. And Rebecca's sisters and brother were all *light skinned*, and she wasn't. She and her siblings were all adopted. I later found out, or either Rebecca was, and she lived with Delores and her sibling's grandmother. However, the story went. Rebecca stood out from the family. In fact, that is why she was so well known. She was teased a lot because of her size and her looks.

I really liked Rebecca. She was nice; but when I was around other kids, I could really be nasty and mean. If I was with some kids in the neighborhood and I happen to see Rebecca at a store or school or somewhere, we'd tease her and call her names, hit her and run to make her chase us. And I would be the main one she would come after. I don't know if it was because I pretended to be her friend one day and talk about her the next, or God wanted me to learn a lesson that would take me through the rest of my life. All I know is that I always got the brunt of the lashings so to speak.

I did feel bad; but at the time we were still doing it, so it just seemed the right thing to do. Now I understand the scripture when it states, "There is a way that seems right to a man but the end thereof is death." (Proverbs 14:12.) Looking back, I sure wish I knew the scripture then. I did not realize how close to death I was. Messing with Big Rebecca was a sure way to die, and I just didn't get that.

One day, after tormenting Rebecca to tears, I ran up on her alone! I guess she had about enough of people teasing her especially me. I had never seen her cry, and I should have taken this as a hint that I had finally gone too far. For a minute, I felt her hurt, and I was hurting for her, but I couldn't stop taunting her. I'd called her all kinds of *big, ugly, black-gorilla-looking, nappy-haired, King-Kong-looking, fat ass, big feet hefa's.* I just couldn't stop the words from coming out, and the crowd around gave me more fuel. I had all my so called friends with me too; but this day, I was alone.

I was in Sister Casoli's church, and none of my *bully* friends were at church with me. There were a few of the *saintly* ones, but not my mischief makers, and those who were there weren't from the area to know how we teased her anyway. Rebecca was sitting across from me in the pews on my left, pointing at me, signifying she was going to get me. She had her fist held up and switched it from her left eye then to her right one, as if to say she was going to blacken my eyes. And all the other kids who were really scared of her looked at me with sympathy. I looked at the door in front of me and the door behind me, trying to anticipated my escape. I reasoned, if I'd got up, Sister Casoli was going to get me for leaving early; but if I stayed put, Rebecca was going to beat me up anyway. I was about to cry.

Finally, Sister Casoli was about to call us up to get our treats as we left out through the door; and I jumped up and ran to the door, grabbed my treat, thanked Sister Casoli, and I took off. I didn't look back; but by the time I made it to the outside gate, Big Rebecca was stomping across the pavement in my direction. She had bolted out the front door when I bolted out the back one. I got out of the gate just as her huge hand reached for me. I ran down the sidewalk across Twenty-First Street to the next sidewalk and hauled it across Twenty-Third Street to Wall Street. I ran so fast that had a car been coming. I would have run through it like a ghost because I would have rather been hit by a car than hit by Rebecca's wrath. I literally didn't stop until I reached my porch.

I jumped, possibly hopped, the five steps in a leap! And when I grabbed the handle of the screen door, to my disappointment, it was locked; and I cried, "Mama!"

My brother jumped to the door mumbling, "What's wrong with chu?"

And all I could gasp was, "Big Re-Bec-ca."

One of our neighbors was in the house with my brother; and when he looked out the door to see Rebecca who had come to a halt by our gate, he said, "Dayumm! I'd have run too if she was after me!" My brother, knowing my MO (modus operandi) by now, said to me, "You *should'na* been messing with her." And I, with disappointment, couldn't say anything. I just knew he was going to beat her down for me.

For two days, I darted in and out of my door, checking to see if Rebecca was lurking about. I was scared to go to stores even for my mama; and I almost got a whooping for it, refusing to go. One day, my mom gave me money to go to the local store and told me I could keep the change. I eventually forgot about Rebecca and let my guard down to make the trip to the store. I jubilantly walked to the store. I turned the corner, and of course, I bumped in to Big Rebecca. In a panic, I turned to run; but she grabbed my shirt, and I hollered and twisted and turned and then she said, "I ain't gone beat you up. I came over to tell you I'm sorry I chased you home." And that was that.

I couldn't believe it was over! It was over! After all I had put her through, she came and apologized to me! I told her I was sorry as well, and we became openly good friends; and I learned that no matter how Rebecca looked, she was much prettier and much of a better person that I had ever been because I acted so ugly and mean to her, and she taught me a valuable lesson that day on that sidewalk, and that was even when things seem to look right ahead, you never know what is lurking around the corner! So always keep your track shoes on!

Patti (Pa-ti)

The story of Patti is a story that I have thought about often in my life. We called her Patti; but in her Mexican culture, her name was pronounced as Pa-ti, and there were times we called her both. She was a nice kid that lived in our area, and I saw her often as I saw any kid I played with on my street. Patti was my friend just the day before all this mess happened, and I was standing there as though I had egg on my face, ready to beat the girl up. Patti was one of the sweetest of students at San Pedro Elementary School and a *neighbor* of mine. She lived on Twenty-Fourth street off Maple, and I lived off Twenty-Third Street and Wall. The two named streets intersected as Twenty-Third Street and Twenty-Fourth Street did if the houses in the neighborhood were removed, and they were the two notorious streets around that little section of working class families and senior citizens that made it a thriving environment. After the events of the day unfold, it was then that I learned that both our brothers were involved in two of the biggest *gangs* in the area; but back then, they were not considered gangs such as the Bloods and Crips. They looked at themselves as *keepers of their castles*. They watched over *their hoods*. Gangs, as we know them today, were not as vicious in our neighborhood. They were mostly kids who drank and took pills and had fights amongst themselves and stole candy from stores or clothes they wanted to wear. It was not all bout drive-by shootings and who can wear what colors and go into what areas. It was just friends who hung with one another on a daily basis and took care of one another. They were more like a pack of wolves than harden criminals.

In the later years, these groups of men and women did change their philosophies in life as they became known as the Flats, The Outlaws (us), Clanton 14, Baby Laws, Lady Laws, Baby Locos, baby Clantons, and so on. As you might can guess, the babies in these groups were the young brothers and sisters of the older kids in the gangs. The graffiti became more prevalent. The fighting became more gang-related, and then, other gang members started coming into our areas; and the changing of the times had begun. But at the time of the incident—if you can call it that— we were far from that, or so I thought because for the most part, we all lived around one another and got along. And usually, when we fought together, it wasn't because we were blacks and Mexicans, it was mainly because someone did something to one of our family members or friends. As I was doing that day on the sidewalk coming from school on San Pedro Street and Washington Boulevard, slapping Pa-ti upside of her head as we both stood there crying. She was crying as I was hitting her, and I was crying because we had been told Dr. Martin Luther King Jr. had been shot and killed. As I was beating this girl up, some-thing inside of me was looking from my eyes, seeing this girl cry. *I recall having an uneasy feeling within me that I had no right, no reason, to be doing this to her*, but I had already hit her, and it was too late to have stopped.

How this all started was, right before the bell rang to let out the kids to go home, the announcement came. The teacher's demeanors had changed. They were walking in and out of the class rooms; and our teacher, I truly can't remember if it was Ms. Caldwell or Ms. Eagleson—both African-American teachers—that told us the bad news because I had them both as teachers. But with tears in her eyes, she made us sit down and delivered that blow. I was nine years old. As the room got quiet, and we all were trying to assess this tragedy, the bell rung, and a group of us, as our custom was, gathered in the play area to wait to see who we would walk home with.

The school was predominantly black in 1968. We were not strangers to racial profiling and racial issues, but we were kids. That was grown up *stuff*; but on that day, all the kids who walked home from school got together and started plotting how we would beat up white kids. I was right in the crowd; and as we were walking through the opened steel (meshed) fence, I recall saying that I would *sock the first white person I see.* Pa-ti was Mexican, and she walked out of the corner store by the school. She was smiling and laughing with her friends, and she looked at me and smiled, and I looked her right in the eyes and socked her in her jaw. Her bubbly laughter ceased, and the look on her face pierced my heart. But when she cried out loud, "What did I do!" All I could muster from my mouth as my tears fell was, "Martin Luther is dead."

And I hit her again in the stomach, and she doubled over, and one of the girls shouted, "Leave her alone! It's not her fault! She didn't do it!"

And when her words hit my ears, I was jerked back into reality. Then I realized that all my so-called *soldiers* who were talking all that crap with me were just standing back, instigating. There were a few of the boys, Barry Stone and Michael Williams, who also hit two boys passing by; but my little crew of girls did nothing. I was the only girl who took it to the extreme. Then I realized that I was crying because I had hurt my friend. She was hurting, and I yelled at her, "Get out of here before I slap you again!"

The girls who were with her never left her side, and it was eight of us to their three. As I reflect back, I have a mad love for those girls. They showed what real friendship was. They could not fight us all, but they didn't leave Patti. And I understand now that was God working in me, to feel Pa-ti's pain like that. I believe now that I think I was more *afraid* of what I was doing than getting in trouble for hitting her; and yes, I did get in trouble when we went back to school. While all this was going on, one of the monitors who watch the kids after school walked out to the sidewalk, hearing all the commotion; and the store owner had stepped out as well and tried to *shoo* us kids away.

That one incident on that *sidewalk* turned our neighborhoods into a little war zone. Word got back to Patti's family and friends about what happened, and unbeknownst to me and *alone* I walked to the liquor store on Maple and Twenty-Third Street. We had three mom and pop stores in the three respective parts of the neighborhood. Mary's store was closest to my house, right on the corner of Twenty-Third and Wall; and the liquor store was on Maple and Twenty-Third west of Mary's, then the *Spanish Store*—as we called it—was on Patti's street Twenty-Fourth and Maple. So leaving my house, I would have to walk in a backwards *L* shape to get to the liquor store. Not thinking of Pa-ti or anything else; but going to buy some candy and going to visit a friend who lived across the street from the store, I pass the big green house where several girls are sitting on the porch. I have passed this house many times before, spoke to the girls, sometimes even talked to them. *Cholas* (girls of Mexican, Latino descent who are down for their Barrios) were not the norm at this time. These were just Mexican girls who like us, didn't take no stuff off just anyone. We grew up with these kids; but as I was passing, I heard someone say, "That's the girl who beat up Pa-ti." I probably should have run right then and there; but before I knew it, the oldest girl—I presumed—was down the steps before I knew it, and she pushed me. I pushed her back, and I ran back and across the street and high-tailed it to go get my brother. I didn't have any sisters, not blood sisters anyway. I don't remember the words that were exchange before we had the pushing match, but I know I had to go get me some help.

When I got to Wall Street, my god-sister Ruby Jewel was outside; and when she saw me run into the house, she had come from across the street to see what was going on. My brother was not home, and I surely couldn't tell my mother to come beat this girl up for me; but I sure wanted to, so I started crying and telling Ruby what happen. As bad as I could be, I never had a problem crying. My teachers always told me I needed to watch my temper; but then when I would get in trouble, I would ball like a baby and learned that tears had power to change things. I used them that day to get Ruby to feel my pain. Ruby was not having it. She took me back around that corner, and we walked up to that house. And that same girl came down, trying to explain what happened; and they started cussing at each other. Before I knew, Ruby had clunked that girl upside the head with her Royal Crown (RC) soda, she casually sipped as she was listening to that girl ranting. The girls from the porch screamed, and people were coming out of the house. And Ruby Jewel still was standing there, waiting to take on any of them. When someone shouted call the police, it was then we left. As we walked away, I looked back and saw Pa-ti who had been there all the time. When our eyes locked, I had an uneasy feeling again inside of me. This was all my fault. Pa-ti seemed to look at me with that same thought in her eyes.

Later that evening, the war began. It wasn't me fighting Pa-ti, or Ruby fighting with the girls, now it was my brother and his friends fighting. Pa-ti's brothers and his friends. All through the neighborhood, all that was heard were feet running. They were jumping from roofs, fences, yelling, and just brawling like it was a real war field. My brother and his friends would chase them, and then Pa-ti's brothers and his friends would retaliate and chase them back. Both sides were fighting toe to toe, *chunking* bottles and rocks. It was crazy. Even the women were in it. As I would peek out the window, seeing all this, I opened the door; and my mother yelled at me to close it. I thought this is all my fault. Pa-ti didn't kill King, and what if she had. All this wasn't going to bring him back.

Eventually, it all died down. The police was called, and they found their way to my door. My brother was in our big, easy chair, trying to wave to me, telling not to give up any name; but I inadvertently told them who Ruby was, and they went to her house and arrested her. Her sister Gloria started calling me a little snitch. She came over to my house the next day, threatening me. She was hurt. I know now 'cause her sister had taken up for me; and I told on her. I felt so bad. She even hit me in my mouth one day, caught me off guard; but my brother got on her, and she backed off me. My mother only scowled and told me I need to keep my tail away from them teenagers. She had no clue I started all that mess until the school contacted her that I would be suspended for fighting Pa-ti. It was hard being ostracized in the hood after that, but I got over it. Ruby, like sister Casoli, came home and forgave me. I told her that the police officer tricked me, saying he just wanted to talk to her. She actually hugged me; and sipping on another RC, she said she still loved me. I learned so many lessons from that day about friendship, codes of the streets, forgiveness, and thinking before reacting. It was a life-changing experience for me, and I stopped hanging around crowds and became a loner. I even went back to apologize to Pa-ti.

One day—as I was over my friend's house who I was going to visit that day—Atlena, we walked to the little Spanish market for her mother. As we were walking in, Pa-ti was walking out. And I looked her square in the eyes again; but this time, the presence that I felt in my heart when I was fighting her arose in me, and I felt myself saying, "I'm sorry for hitting you."

And in her bubbly way, she said, "It's okay. I just didn't understand why you were so mad."

I just shrugged my shoulders. I guess looking back, I didn't think if I tried to explain that impact Dr. King had on our lives, and how we as black people had so much hope and faith in his work to get us *over*. She wouldn't get it, so I just walked away and went to where Atlena stood, paying for the items her mom wanted. As Pa-ti was walking away, I called out to her, "Hey! Pa-ti, are they selling firecrackers over there still?"

She stopped and turned around and said, "Yes, we have some." And I knew then things were back to normal.

I know that what happen that day could have gotten someone killed. The reason I added this story to my compilation of stories is because it shows how bad decision making and bad choices, split decisions can change your life in an instant. Had this happen in this day and age, those young men and women would not have been throwing rocks and bottles or trying to fight with fists. They would have been shooting and stabbing one another. The mentality was so very different that day, April 4, 1968, but all across the world, there were riots and racial breakouts that Dr. King would not have approved of at all. And I fell right into it, hook, line, and sinker. I am so grateful to God that even then—as a young mischievous child on the sidewalk trying to express my hurt and pain—he interceded for Pa-ti and me and taught us both valuable lessons, one of courage for her and one of deliverance for me.

The Bouncing Ball Man

(Dedicated to Patricia Cummings)

In a world of make-believe and fairy tales, it amazes me that there are so many real crazy *goings ons in this world.* I know in the Bible it tells of demon-possessed people who did strange things and saw strange things, and miracles happened that seemed strange. People walking on water, snakes talking, and angels appearing—stories in the Bible that we have come to believe in and accept as true and non-fictional.

This story about the bouncing ball man is a story that I never knew whether it was true or not. I know how it affected me as a child, hearing about it; and how I never forgot it. As the story went, he would bounce a ball and intrigue young women by it; and once he was close enough on them, he would attack the woman (or young girls) and kill them by strangulation or with a knife. It was a horrifying story especially to young girls my age hearing of it. When I first heard of it, I had to be in the age bracket of eight years old to ten. I was very young. I was over my friend Baba's (Bay-Bay) house one day after not going straight home from school, as I was supposed to have done. My Mom knew I went over to her house after school sometimes; but this day, I didn't tell her I would, so I stayed a little longer than I intended too. In hindsight, I believe this is why I *accidently* overheard one of *the most horrific stories of my life.*

Baba and I were sitting on her front porch when we saw her eldest sister and one of her friends walk up. We had been in the house playing records and eating and just talking about the boys we liked

41

and basically just passing time. Her big sister *Tricia* was talking with Bobbi Stevenson who lived next door. Tricia and Bobbi were both good looking girls. Bobbi had a younger sister, Joann, who also went to school with Baba and me, but she was in the house this day. So as they were standing there talking, we went out to the gate to listen. They were talking about the bouncing ball man and the women he had killed. Surely, we were not expecting to get an earful of that!

They were talking about a man who was going around killing *anybody* who got in his path as he was bouncing his ball. *He'd walk down the street bouncing the ball; and before he passed you, he'd catch you off guard and kill you leaving you on the sidewalk dead.* We joined in the conversation, asking all kind of little kid questions such as, "for real? *Where?"* Just questions that annoyed them. Then Tricia looked at me and asked, "Arlene, how you getting home?"

I lied and said that my brother Charlie was coming to get me. To which she remark, "Charlie and Bobo and them just went to basketball practice."

I must have look scared because when I asked Baba to walk me halfway home, she laughed and said, "Uh-huh." I was scared too. Bobbi laughed and told Tricia she was going home, and Tricia looked at Baba and smirk, "Baba, come on and let's walk this girl home."

So Tricia and Baba and I walked across the street. They lived on Twentieth and Stanford. That was a pretty good ways from my house. I would have to walk up to Twenty-Third Street and then down to Wall Street. We were talking eight or nine blocks at least; but once we made it to Twenty-Second Street, I told Tricia I could make it from there, and I took off running. It was getting dark, and I had no intentions on getting strangled or killed that day. Looking back, I should have stayed and went to All People's Community Center where my brother had gone to play ball; but fear did not allow me to think straight.

After I made it home, just as quick as the fear had come, it left. Once I smelled my mom cooking and seen her face, I knew I was safe. I never heard anything more about the bouncing ball man, except on occasions. We kids would try to scare one another, if we stayed out too late playing, and it was getting dark, but I never trusted anybody. I saw walking the streets bouncing a ball. I would run the other way or cross streets. As I grew older, I realized that there were so many stories of this nature that were told over and over again. Stories of women stealing kids to eat them, killed them, or just burn them. There was one story about La Llorona (the crying lady). I had heard that story from my Mexican friends. It was about the lady who drowned her kids in the Mexico Ocean, and she cried day and night over their deaths. And if you get near her, she will cause harm to you. There were so many versions, but all of them frightening. My friend Peewee's little sister Peaches used to come to school talking about *haints* and ghosts that would slap you in the face and then say, "There go some red apples." It sounds silly to believe now; but back then as a child, that was spooky. There were stories of Mary widow, the pig lady, and yes, even the wolf man. So when I heard wolf man Jack on the radio howling and later on the variety show *the Midnight Special*, I could not understand why they hadn't locked this monster up!

Patrica (Tricia) is no longer with us, but I had to include her in one of my stories because she was such an integral part of my life. This story actually happened. I can't remember the actual time and date, but I could not talk about my life without incorporating the bouncing ball story. I don't know if she ever realized that there was an actual man name Raymond W. Clemmons who had killed seven women, and he used to bounce a ball. When I researched this story and found this information, chills ran through my body. There actually was a real killer who was called the Bouncing Ball Man. He was known for killing in the areas of Hoover and Mount Vernon and not too far from where we lived. In an excerpt from ourweekly.com article, it read, *"The scary part of the story was the description of the ball striking the pavement. It created a distant thump that became louder as he approached your street. According to our story tellers, the bouncing noise throughout the neighborhood meant death"* (William Covington, 09/25/2014).

Bo Diddly

My mother always tried to instill in us to love life and to pursue God. She never really broke it down to us that Jesus needs to be our personal Savior; but she let it be known that *we were going to church, to school, and work around the house.* She always seemed to be smiling, laughing, and helping people: qualities I never knew to respect in her until I was grown myself.

She called my brother Charlie "Bo Diddly"—why, I never knew—and she called me "Sally Mop Handle" (later, I learned because I was so skinny). I know she had a sense of humor. We were her only kids, and she taught us to love each other and watch out for each other. Bo was around when songs were sang like, "Bo diddly bo diddly have you heard…" We were six years apart. I came along when Mustang Sally was popular in 1965; and after understanding the songs better, I saw how they fit our personalities so well. Charlie was slow moving and quiet. I moved fast and was loud.

I watched my mama's ways. I watched how she treated people, and how she had good come-back jokes when she was having a good time with her friends. She gave hugs and fed people (sometimes we barely had food). People just loved being around her. My dad used to call her Pig, and he would say, "Pig, where the money I gave you for the shoes?" and she would tell him she helped someone with it; and he would be upset, but he never cursed her. He would just shake his head. My brother and I got along fairly well. We were all we had; and being six years apart, he was protective over his baby sister.

My mother also knew I could be conniving too. She would watch how we play together and see how I manipulated my brother into doing things for me. On several occasion she had told me that if I weren't careful, my little games would backfire on me. I shunned her off. She said, "One of these days, you gone call for Bo, and he ain't gone be there." I could not fathom that. Even after he later died, I just could not believe that my big brother had left me here alone. Three or four times a month, I would do something to catch him off guard, so he could run to my rescue from making big splashes in the water as though I had fallen to make-believe crying, as though someone had hurt me. And each time he would bust in the bathroom door or run to the front door to see about me, and I would *bust* up laughing. All he would say is, "Stop playing, girl."

One day, I was walking home from school; and I was coming through the park on Trinity and Twenty-Fourth Street. I got the notion to start crying really loud. I saw some guys playing on the basketball court and just knew Charlie was over there because he always was on that court; but this day, it was only Val Blue and Andrew and Butch (Earl Williams). When they saw and heard me, they stopped playing and ran over to the fence and began questioning me and coming to check on me. I was so outdone, all I could do was run away from them before they could come around the fence to check on me. Butch was the eldest of the three, and he said, "Girl, you need to stop playing like that."

Once I was out of their reaches, I could see through the screen door that the wood door to our house was opened. So I figured Bo was home. I was about to get him good. About fifty yards away, I opened my mouth wide and waled. I know if Butch could have got to Charlie first, he would have told on me. But he couldn't, and I was too close to the house. My brother ran out the door so fast and grabbed me. I was holding my face, and he pulled my hands down, and I let out the biggest laugh. But what I wasn't expecting was for my mother to be home, and she came to the porch and told me, "Get yo' ass in here fo' I give you something to cry fo'!" I knew if I passed her she still was going to swing on me, but I had to get in there, so I ran up the porch steps and dipped in my shoulders and sure enough she tried to smack me. I couldn't help but laugh. I almost ran into the door trying to avoid her.

But the one lesson that taught me well was when I was hit by a car. I was coming from school walking with Ava Farley on San Pedro

Street. We were always walking home together if I was going straight home. Ava very seldom would deviate from her route leaving school, but I on the other would do it in a minute. As we were walking, we met up with Everett Evans and Eric Cartwright, and we all started playing around, and they were trying to catch us. Everett reached for me, and I giggled myself free from him but snatched the wrong way and a little too hard and went into moving traffic. Before I knew it, I had been hit and jumped up of shock and ran down the street. People were chasing me. I was crying for real, and Ava was crying. People were stopping in their cars, trying to give me help. Freddie caught up with me. He was the one driving. He was my brother's friend Bobo, big brother. I had seen that thunderbird around in the neighborhood so many times, never would I have thought I would almost lose my life behind it; or should I say in front of it.

Once the initial shock of the accident was over, and Freddie was standing in front of me asking me if I were okay, that temper flared up. I tried to snatch away from him, but he wouldn't let me go. People were still yelling for the police and ambulance to be call, but I told Freddie I didn't want to go to the hospital. I talked my way out of going, and he let me go. Ava and I walked back up to San Pedro Street so she could go home, but I went over BaBa's house. I don't remember why. I don't know if I thought if I go home, I would be in trouble. I just really don't know. But I remember telling Baba I had got hit by a car, and she didn't believe me at first until I showed her my scrapes. After a while, I did go home. I probably was walking around with a concussion and not thinking straight.

It was almost three or four hours before I went home. I even went by Ava's house and remember her asking me had I been home yet. I went home finally after talking with Ava, and my mom wasn't home, so I went to Mr. JP's house to look for her. As I approached his door, I could hear them laughing and talking loud. Mr. JP was a big man who would remind one of James Earl Jones. He was always cooking and having parties. I didn't know it until I was older that he was *special* (today they call it gay), but he was a good person. I knocked on the door and asked for my mother; and as she brought her *happy* self out, I told her that *I had been hit by a car*. She didn't believe me and told me *to go on home and to stop practicing lying.* She really didn't believe me, and I was too tired to put up a fight. As soon as I went inside of the house, I went straight to bed. I was not feeling good at all.

Later that evening, I remember lying in bed moaning and groaning. I couldn't get up. My brother thought I was playing again and came in there to chastise me; but when he saw the tears flowing down my face and the painful look I had in my eyes, he asked me what was wrong with me and then I told him how Freddie hit me with his car. He pulled the covers back and looked at my leg, and it had swollen three times its normal size. He knew then I wasn't playing; and when I told him the kind of car it was, he got mad. He ran to go get my mother. Charlie was about to be eighteen. I was in my last year of six grade. He had a reputation for not being afraid to fight, but I didn't want him to think it was all Freddie's fault, so I added that I was playing on the sidewalk and slipped as his car was passing by. He was still upset, but he let it go. By the time he returned with my mom, she rushed in there and looked at me and said, "I should have known something was wrong when she was in here, sleep so early."

She had come home before Bo did and looked in on me. So she went and got us a ride because my dad wasn't home yet, and *cellphones* were not a thought back then and took me to the *General Hospital.* We grew up calling it that, but it was the Los Angeles USC Medical Center. We went there for *everything.* After the doctor ordered ex-rays, he told my mother that I had a bug in my leg; and what he say that for, I must had cried loud enough for the whole hospital to hear me. I was crying, "I don't want a bug in my leg! I don't want a bug in my leg." How was I to know he was talking about an infection? He explained that the impact from the car cut my right leg; and when I rolled on the tar, gravel or some type of debris must have caused the infection and that's what infected my leg beside the very fact of body meeting machine. I had worn a dress that day. *Mama always told me to wear clean underwear, 'cause you don't never know what could happen.*

I stayed in the hospital a week and a few days. I thought I was going to lose my leg because they hospitalized me, but they performed a surgical procedure that required a skin grafting. The cut on my leg was a plug out of my leg, and it wouldn't close. They told me they would take the skin off a place where it would not show, which was my behind. I started wailing all over again. I took that as they were going to cut off half my butt! My mother was too through. She told me to straighten up my face and stop crying, so the doctor finished explaining and assured me I wouldn't even miss the skin. I was traumatized, but I learned to take myself home from school and to stop playing around so much, and that being the girl who cried wolf is not a good person to be.

I was a changed person, when I got out of the hospital, I stayed out of school a month; and I never took a joke too far ever again. I learned it's okay to laugh and play but never at the expense of others. It turned out that Freddie and his crew who was with him that day had all been drinking and getting high. He was really glad I didn't go to the hospital or that the police came because if they had, they all would have gone to jail or prison. So I guess I learned my lessons, and he could count his blessings. One of my schoolmates, Melinda Lopez, lived near my friend Raymond Whitten; and she had gone to school telling people how I flew up in the air and landed on the street. At first, I was mad because I took it as they were laughing at me; but she said, "No, for real you went up in the air, and you came back down, and you got up and ran." I couldn't stay mad. She was only telling it as she saw it. My teachers always told me to watch my temper, so I let it go. But in hindsight, I would have loved to see that moment from Melinda's eyes. She continued, "I thought you were dead!"

Everything happened so fast that day. I can't explain how I felt, but looking back, I can't say that the devil had it in for me because he knew I would grow up to be an advocate for Christ, and he was trying to take me out, or that it goes with my beliefs that we can cause our own problems in our lives by our choices and decisions we make. Oftentimes, we say it is the devil's fault; but I have come to believe that it be our own faults. The devil just sits back and gets the glory, but I believe we change our own destinies. And the moment I misstepped off that sidewalk on San Pedro Street, I had a hand in changing mine.

The Pot Top

I was eleven years old attempting to be thirty. Not that all thirty-year-olds go around popping pills and drinking wine and smoking cigarettes and having sex with grown men. Well, the sex came later; but at that tender age, I was not far from it, and it was not my choice. But I just seem to attract men and boys who wanted to feel and touch and kiss all over me. When I first saw a red devil, I knew what it was. I had learned about them in school. I had people around me taking them every day. Technically, they were called *seconals*; but in the hood, they were called *stumblers*. I saw people, teen-agers, and old folks walking around high off them pills, holding on to fences and running into buildings trying to drive under the influence of those pills. It looked fun; and sometimes, it was funny to watch them. Pills were high on the list of items to get high-off of during that time.

I wasn't a bad kid. I was mischievous, and I would try just about anything especially if there was a *dare*. I played with other little kids, and I did as I was told. I respected my elders and went on errands for grown-ups too lazy to go to the store for themselves. There was one old guy, every time he wanted me to go to the store for him, he would want to grab me and try to kiss me. He could barely walk and was just as nasty as he wanted to be. I would steal his money every chance I got. He knew too if he told my mother, I would tell her he tried to touch me. I just had a natural instinct for survival within me. I learned later it was not a good game to play, but it was who I was. He left me alone too.

I had what is considered a *normal childhood*: two parents and both in the home, a brother, no dog or cat. I owned a Susy Homemaker oven, Barbie dolls, the first Black Barbie Julia, and my hot wheels set. So when I wasn't doing grown-up things, smoking, drinking, cussing, and fighting, I played with *my little girl things.* I don't remember exactly when I was molested. I just know that I was, and it lasted for what seemed like forever. But through it all, I had something inside of me that just refused to be hurt by it, and I used everything in me to turn it around. Some studies have shown that some victims enjoy what is happening to them after a while, and maybe that happened to me because I began using it for my advantage. This story isn't about molestation, so I will spare the statistics. I just want the reader to know just what kind of kid this story is about. During this time being molested, I was giving pills and booze and cigarettes. I could basically get whatever I wanted as long as I didn't tell, and I fell into that trap.

One day, my brother had come home; and he had a big bash of red devils and hid them in the clothes' closet. I was on my bed drawing and acted like I didn't notice what he was doing. Soon as he closed the front door, I was up and in that bag. It was a sandwich bag full of red devils in little pieces of foil. Back then, they were three in a roll. That meant you get three pills rolled up in aluminum foil. They were going for the price of five dollars a roll if that much; but whatever it was, it was a lot of money for the era. So I took three out of the bag and went looking for my friend Brenda Williams. I ran through the park and up Trinity Street to Twenty-First street where she lived. I had to cross Twenty-Third Street to get to her house, and she was home. I showed her what I had, and we left her house. We decided to stop at the boys and girls club Catholic Youth Organization (CYO), and went into the bath room and *popped the pills!* Then later, we ran into her sister Annie Bea; and they wanted some too and was asking me *where did I get them from,* and *how did I get them.* We all ended up being so high at the CYO. Everyone there noticed. Brenda and I stayed at the CYO, trying to play pool laughing and giggling when we missed or couldn't hit the balls; but Annie Bea and her friend went off somewhere else. The teen counselors were looking at us funny. We left. We knew we were getting too much attention.

We were already known as the two little rebels. We didn't dance to anyone's music but our own.

On another occasion, my brother confronted me about his *sack*. He wanted to know if I had been in it, and I told him that I hadn't. But he didn't believe me and told me to stay out of his bag, that it wasn't his; and he had to pay that money back. Then I guess he realized he was fussing at me about some drugs and asked me *what was I doing with them anyway?* Well right before he had come in, I had checked to see if he left them in the same spot. They were, and I took only two rolls out. That was six pills. Three for me, and three for Brenda. I had heard him coming in and jumped on my bed as though I was coloring. He probably suspected I had been into something because I was just too calm. So again, I went to find Brenda; and as I was leaving, she was walking through the park, coming to my house. So I met her halfway and told her what I had, and we went to find some water to take the pills. We went to the coach's building to go to the water faucet and took turns taking our pills. We didn't take all three, but I took two, and I believe Brenda did as well. So we went to play tether ball; and as we are moving around and jumping up and down, the pills bust inside of us. We both start acting like we were walking on clouds.

Brenda and I were at the park across the street from my house, Trinity Park; and we'd manage to walk to the coach's office. We were going to check out the Carrom board game. That's a game where each opponent gets a wooden stick a piece and try to shoot little checker like circles in one of four corners. As the coach was talking to us, he kept asking us if we were alright. His name was Coach Ben. He was a nice looking man. He had begun to make us nervous, so we just said forget it, and we laughed leaving out of his office just laughing. He followed us out the door; and just when Brenda and I was going to figure out what else we could do, my mother called me from the porch.

Everything was funny to me and Brenda. It was as though we had smoked weed instead of dropped them stumblers, and were we stumbling. Brenda told me she as going to go home, and she started off in the direction of her house. How she got home, I don't know to this day; but as for me, I had to try to walk a straight line to that porch. The last thing Brenda said to me was, "Arlene, your mama gonna beat your ass." Even that was funny, and I didn't do whooping well at all.

As I got to the hill nearest my house, the full effect of the pills exploded in me. It was as though they were on a time release, and the second one activated itself by itself. I was trying to walk straight as I could as I approached my mama. Then she asked me, "What the hell wrong with you?"

And I replied, "Nuttin'."

Then she told me, "Go down to Ernestine's house and get my pot top and bring yo' ass right back here!" Ernestine was a friend of the family who called my mother mama as well. It was her husband who had me always running for my life, making me do *womanly* things with him, and in a twist of fate—if that's what you can call it—Ernestine ended up with my daddy. It was all crazy, and I hated going to her house because of her husband.

Now as I can recall, I tried to walk straight as I could to Ernestine's house. It was probably not even a 100 yards, fifty at the most. I felt myself swaying back and forth, but I was stepping like a soldier. I just knew it. If they had World Star back then, I would have gone viral. There was a construction crew working on a building in the middle of the block. It was going to be a senior citizen's apartment building. It was to be the first of many to erect throughout our neighborhoods and throughout the city. I made it Stine's house, and she too wanted to know if anything was wrong with me. Again, I lied that there wasn't; but actually, it wasn't a lie because I thought I was just fine. In fact, I was feeling mighty fine. I didn't have a worry in the world. She walked outside with me, and I could hear her saying things like, "Lena, you high?"

Her porch had three huge cement steps. I made it up them; but coming down them, I drop the pot top. It rolled toward the hole the construction man was in. As I went to bend to pick it up, one of the construction men in the hole caught the pot top and handing it to me, asked me, "Are you okay? Are you on something?"

And I could hear Stine in the background fussing, "Hell yeah, she just as high as she want to be!"

When I reached for the pot top, I almost fell forward as though I would into the hole; and the men sang out, "Whoaaa!" and one of them jumped up from the little ditch and came to steady me.

I said, "Thank you."

I started off again. Unbeknownst to me the men, and Ernestine all stood there watching me and that pot top fight our way to my porch. Every two steps, I took that damn pot top, found a way to fall! From Stine's house to mine, it took me fifteen minutes to make it home, thirty yards away. I finally made it home, and the only thing I remembered from that point was walking up handing my mom the pot top that fell again out of my hands as I was trying to give it to her. My uncle Chico told me what happened next.

My uncle Chico later told me when I slept it off, that my mother had watched me stumble and wobble all the way up and back with that pot top. He said there were a lot of people watching and laughing at me, struggling with that pot top. He had asked my mom to let him go get me, and she had told him, "Oh I'ma get her alright," and that when I handed her the pot top she commenced to whooping my butt. I didn't drop the pot top. She swooped it out my hand! She had gone in the house while I was walking to Stine's house to get a belt and came back out to wait for me. I hadn't felt a thing.

That battle on that sidewalk with that pot top was one for the history books. I was teased about that for a long time. Needless to say that, that was not the last time I got high. In fact, I even moved up to stronger drugs and ended up in prison behind drugs and alcohol eventually in my lifetime; but it is memories like that that I hold dear to my heart especially now that my mother is deceased and my Uncle Chico and so many who witnessed that fiasco that day. I am just grateful to God that I have been able to come to my senses and that I can write and laugh about it all today. Every time I drop a pot top, it takes me back to that long walk on that sidewalk on Twenty-Third and Wall Street.

The Day I Hated My Brother

M y brother is dead now, but five kids and over twenty grandkids later, his memory and his legacy live on. Charlie Ray Richardson, a name with the sound of greatness but short lived to the age of thirty-seven years old. Sometimes I can smell his body odor, his breath, and still see him in movies. He is Wesley Snipes, Don Cheadle, and Omar Epps all in one respectively. We only had each other. Sibling wise that is. He had a brother by his daddy but not with the same mother. I only had Charlie. He was my *brudda*. I loved my brudda. I couldn't say brother when I was a kid. My mom told me once, and I gave him the name brudda.

There was not anything he couldn't do. He ran track, played basketball, football. He swam, fought well, and was popular with the guys and the girls. When girls found out he was my brother, they were so nice to me; and when the bullies found out he was my brother, they were nice to me too. And because I knew he was my brother, I could be *not so nice* to others. "I'mma go get my brother,' was golden to me." It was my American Express card. I smile as I can hear my mother's voice saying, "You and your brudda gone get yall asses whooped one day."

I was always calling on my brother to fight for me until he figured it out that his baby sister was a bully. Then I had to fend for myself unless it was really, really serious. Other than that, he made me fight my own battles. I didn't realize he was getting *hood reports* on me. People were coming to him, telling him how I was acting and starting things, little things like that. I say that with tongue in cheek, but I was regulating in the hood, and I wasn't even in Junior High School yet.

My father raised my brother from a young buck. I believe he was seven, if not younger, when my daddy began courting my mom. Charlie knew his daddy, Booker Ree Richardson. My mother just moved on with her life and left him in Arizona. I came along in 1958. I was my mom and dad's own, but my dad never treated him differently. My daddy took good care of us. He worked hard to make us comfortable at home, and we didn't want for any necessities, but things we *desired* could wait, or we had to get them on our own. Charlie was very protective of me. He was quiet, but he could get riled up if someone pissed him off. I had the opportunity to see him in action a few times. I saw him fight at parties and in the park by our house. When he got on drugs, I saw how he changed from meek and mild to wild and bold. I don't know when he actually took his first drink or drug, but I think that it was this combination that put a gap between him and my dad. I always thought he was a square. I loved Charlie. He caught me with some of my friends in the backyard smoking, and he popped me upside the head. That hurt my feelings so badly I cried. He had never hit me before, not even if we were playing because he knew how sensitive I was. I think I cried every time he looked at me that day.

We moved to Los Angeles from Blythe, California. I was born in Blythe, and Charlie was born in Stansfield, Arizona. After leaving Arizona, my mother met my dad in Blythe; and they became involved. She lived there until I was four years old. My grandmother and my cousin Charles lived in Blythe with my aunt Agrie Ree (all of whom are deceased now), and they were the only reasons we would periodically visit Blythe throughout the years once we moved to LA. I was about eleven or twelve years old when my mom and I had to go to Blythe to check on my grandmother who had begun to have sick spells. My mom had broken her leg somehow, and she was in a cast, but I didn't want to leave. I asked her if I could stay, but she told me there was no way she was going to leave me there. So we ended up getting on the greyhound bus; and against my will, we went to Blythe. We were not there. It seemed less than a day maybe two, that someone called my mama and told her she had to get home quick. My dad was in the hospital. When she got off the phone and told us the news, I started crying. Once before my dad had taken Charlie and me to the theater to see a movie, he fell out clutching his heart, and I just knew it was a heart attack. But when mama got off the phone, she look annoyed more than upset that daddy was having a heart attack. Then she dropped the bomb, "That damn boy done hit Roger in the head with a bat. Well, damn would a heart attack have been better." I was so angry. The tears stopped flowing.

My aunty, we called her Ainee. She said, "Ah nah Daws. What happened?" she asked.

Mama replied, "Probably high off that damn dope," and she added, "Ever since he been messing with that mess he been acting a damn fool."

Now I knew what dope was. I had stolen his pills from him before, but I thought to myself, *I didn't know it would make you act crazy!* And the next thing I knew, we were back on the Greyhound bus headed back to Los Angeles. My mother was going through it, but she never showed her weakness. She was always a pillar of strength. One thing I did learn though as my Ainee had said to my mother, having a round trip ticket is the only way to travel, and I learned that the hard way in my later years.

When we got home, one of my dad's friends had come to pick us up. He said that Charlie was gone, and daddy was in the hospital. (I cried again.) At that moment, I felt a hatred for my beloved brudda. *How could he do this to daddy? After all daddy had done for him, what was he thinking? He had bought him clothes, fed him, given him money, and he hit him with a bat!* I just didn't understand how all this could have happened.

Several hours after, we'd been home, we found out that Earl Williams "Butch" had snatched the bat from Charlie and threw Charlie to the ground and was whooping his ass. Butch was much older than Charlie, and he was one of the older brothers of my friend Brenda, but Butch was no joke. I gloated inwardly. I was glad somebody was able to tame his butt. Butch didn't really just beat him down. He just stopped my brother from swinging again then they scuffled, and Butch made Charlie leave. Apparently, Charlie had been drinking all day and taking them pills and was getting into it with a few people that day. When my dad came home from work and tried to talk to him, he turned on my dad and grabbed that bat. The pills and alcohol had him in a bad state of mind. When my dad saw that he could not control Charlie, he turned to walk away; and that they say is when he swung on my dad. He could have killed him. I am grateful he didn't, and he could have gone to prison for a very long time. Later, the doctor's told my dad if he had been closer to the front of his head he would have been dead or in a coma for a very long time. God blessed them both.

My dad lived and no charges were brought against my brother. He received a complimentary ass-whooping by Butch; and eventually, all was forgiven. But he and my dad never rekindle the relationship they had once had. The trust was gone; and my dad basically told him if he had the nerve to hit him once, he could do it again. My brother swore that he'd never do that again, but it was not the same between them. My dad stopped providing for him. He still ate and slept at the house but as far as giving him extra money. He told him to find a job. I hated my brother for that moment. Some of the people had stopped talking to him for what he had done, and I tried to avoid him too, but I loved my brudda. I couldn't hate him. We never really talked about why he felt he had to do that because it was evident. It was the alcohol and drugs, and alcohol is a drug too. My mother, she talked bad to Charlie. I know God himself wanted to come rescue my brother from her wrath. She talk to him bad; but in a way, that made him understand. *You just don't do those kind of things to the ones who love you.* Everyone eventually started back-treating Charlie like they always had, showing him love and kicking it with him. I know in my heart he felt bad about what he did. I know if he could have changed that evening on the sidewalk. He would have. My dad never not opened the door for him. Even when my dad moved out of the house and into the projects, my brother was welcomed to his house until the day he died; and when my brother died, my dad cried the hardest.

Russell (Roo-Sell)

Cookie and I were not the best of friends, but we were friends. Her baby sister and I were *friends*. Atlena and I were the ones who were the same ages and in some of the same classes and acted like the little kids we were. Cookie hung with Cheryl Farley, my best friend Ava Farley's big sister; and we three younger girls hung around them trying to be big girls. They were known as the Releford girls. That was their last names. We all went to church together and school and to the local boys and girls clubs, the CYO and All Peoples. The CYO was in our neighborhood, but All Peoples was (and still is) near our school, San Pedro Elementary School. I liked being around Cookie. She was fun to hang with and didn't mind if I smoked cigarettes with her, and she could sew her butt off. So I learned a lot from Cookie. I even learned that she like a boy who lived across the street from her. His name was Junior, and he rode a *bike,* not many young black men rode a motorcycle in our neighborhood during this time. He had the deepest dimples ever; and all the girls around him fell in love with him, all the girls, even the Mexican girls too. I had a crush on him too, but there was another young man who would visit junior, and he was so *pretty* to me. He had long hair and hazel green eyes, and I just adored him. His name was Russell. We sat in the window of Cookie's parent's apartment and would wait to see them. Almost every single day, we would wait to get a glimpse of them.

We couldn't wait until Junior rode up on his motorcycle, looking like the black knight on that bike. We'd walk the sidewalks on Twenty-Third Street just to get a *look* of him on his bike or see him sitting on his grandmother, *Mama Stella's* porch. Sometimes, we would only catch him rolling up slowly, engine off coasting to park his bike. Even that was thrilling. School-girl crushes can be serious. A lot of people hung out at Mama Stella's place. She lived in a big Victorian-style house on Twenty-Third Street and Maple that had a huge porch, and everyone, it seemed came by to sit on that porch. There was a liquor store on the north side of the street, and it was a popular little store in the area that was owned by Junior's friend, Norman's parents. Norman would always tease us about our *li'l-girl crushes* as he called them. We used to go in the store and play around with him. When Cookie go in to get cigarettes (that's when anyone could buy them), and his brother Jeff—who was also fine as wine— would be in there cracking jokes with us too. Susi, their little sister, was a beautiful girl as well. They all were fun to talk with and kept us laughing. They knew if Junior and Russell were to come in the store we would be somewhere nearby. We would be following in next. When I locked my eyes on Russell, I forgot about Junior; and there was no looking back.

Russell Bryant was the sparkle in my eyes. I was in love at the first sight of him. I'd forgotten all about my dolls, my playmates, and my friends. I was so distracted. I had a driving force within me to marry this man, and that's exactly what he was, a man! Junior and he was much older than I. Cookie was a teenager, but I was thirteen. I told Cookie and Atlena that I had plans to marry Russell, and they thought that was the funniest thing, but I was seriously in love. I would run home from school and just wait for Russell to come to the store, get off work, go to mama's Stella's house, or just wait to see him walking down the street.

For the most part, Cookie and I would just sit in her living room window and wait for them. Atlena became annoyed with me because I didn't want to play with her anymore. Sometimes we even fought because she became jealous of Cookie and my relationship. She would try to stop me from coming in the house when I would come over until Cookie would shove her away from the door then they would start scuffling. From Cookie's window, we had a direct view of Mama Stella's house. By now, both men were used to us whis- tling out the window or hollering their names to get their attention.

Sometimes, they would be together, or it would be one or the other. Cookie would sit in the window and call me if she saw Russell, and I would take a turn and call her if I saw Junior. We were intensified about these guys.

How I came to really get to know Russell is through his dad Moses. Mr. Moses would come on Wall Street to play the horses with my mom and dad. They had *bookie-joints* on our street and at Mama Stella's. So Russell would come by sometimes looking for his dad, and he even played the horses at times too! I didn't see him as a man. *I just saw him.* One time, he knocked on our door looking for his dad, and I nearly fainted when I opened the door and was looking into those eyes of his up close and very personal. I didn't care that up close, I noticed he had a few teeth missing; and he looked much older than I thought. I was mesmerized. I don't even remember if I told him where his dad was or not. All I remember is that I knew I had to run around to Cookie's and fast to let her know what had just happened. My heart had beat as though drums were being played inside of me. As I had left to go to Cookie's, I made it up in my mind right then and there I was going to let him know about my undying love for him. So I went and wrote a letter to Russell, and I folded it up and ran around to Cookie and Atlena's house. I was going to catch him coming home because they lived on Twenty-Fourth Street and Maple. I never got a chance to give it to him. Not one Releford was home. I left disappointedly and hoping I would run into him on my way home. I ran back home. But the meeting didn't happen, at least not that day.

One day, Junior and Russell were walking right under the window of the building Cookie lived in, and I dropped a letter right in front of Russell. I had kept that letter with me, professing my undying love for him. I had written several and finally had the nerve to deliver one. Once I did that, an overwhelming feeling of embarrassment just covered my whole being. I dodged him for a month. I felt as though my world had just been crushed with a giant boulder like a ball and chain smashing into a dilapidated home. I felt dumb.

Cookie, who real name was Cemira, ended up dating Junior, and they had a long relationship. I lost contact with them both after a while, as my life took on a drastic change and all the crushes and childhood-*woozies* played out. I learned later in life that once you go after something you love or want to do, you have to keep that same enthusiasm that you used to get it, to keep it or continue doing it. Once the fire goes out, sometimes it is hard to re-kindle it. That was not the case with Russell and I, but I think about this time in my life when I need to draw strength to keep motivated and enthusiastic about something. This was a good lesson in my life for many *things* to come.

I didn't realize it at all that I was *jailbait* for Russell. All I knew was that I was in love, and I knew he was older than me but not by *thirteen* years! He looked so young. I learned that he had those eyes and that hair because he was *Creole.* He was coffee with a lot of cream with a touch of roasting from the sun. He had an accent (his family spoke French), and as he was funny to talk with. I had assumed by the way he interacted with the people around him. I couldn't think straight for wanting this man, and it wasn't just about his looks. It was something deeper than that, inside of me pulling me toward this man; and I would soon find out why.

Mama Stella' porch and our front porch were gathering sites for our streets respectively. The crowds were interchangeable at times, but each porch always had a crowd. If they weren't on our porch, you more than likely would find them on Mama Stella's porch. I came home from school one day just running along the sidewalk being a kid and I reached my porch I saw Russell getting out of the car with Uncle Jeff and Uncle Red. They were not my real uncles, but they used to say call them uncle cause mister made them feel too old. Uncle Jeff was my friend Gilda's dad. Gilda and I played together when he would bring his kids over, and we went to Sister Casoli's church together also. They both were good friends of my dad. They acted as though they were brothers. Upon seeing Russell get out of that car, I almost fainted. I wanted to turn around and run back the way I had come, but it was too many people on their porch. They probably would have thought I had lost my mind too. When he straighten up and saw me, he smiled and said, "Hi.'

I spoke to him and darted up the porch steps and bolted through our door. By this time, I had written him so many letters. It was too embarrassing, and I learned that his family didn't call him Russell. They called him by his Creole name *Roo-sell*. That made him even more intriguing to me. I thought everyone and their mothers knew now how much I cared for Roo-sell.

After I had composed myself, I walked back unto the porch to get another look at Russell, but I pretended to be going to the store. As I walked by him, he spoke to me again, asking me where I was going; and I told him, but I kept walking. I overheard him telling Uncle Red that he was about to go home. As I crossed the street, I heard uncle Red shout, "Don't have me waiting for you in the morning!"

And I look back over my shoulder as Russell stopped to reply in that broken French voice of his, "No, man, I don't do dat. I need dat job!" And he laughed and turned around to walk away. I was taking it all in. The store was only twenty yards away, but I was stalling to watch him.

Then Lisa come out of nowhere, calling his name. "Roo-sell! Come 'ere, my baby! Where you go?" Lisa was Hawaiian. She was the *crazy* one in the bunch who lived a few doors down from me. She ran off her porch and grabbed Russell and gave him a big ol' kiss right in the mouth! The street was busy that day and a lot of kids and grown-ups were out. Uncle Red and Uncle Jeff was laughing, and some of her family members were as well. They all thought it was funny, but I didn't. They all were bantering and joking, and I was devastated. I walked on to the store like I really had money, so instead, I detoured toward Cookie and Atlena's house.

I really didn't have intentions to go over to their apartment house; but in a daze, I found myself walking in that direction. I just couldn't get that image of Lisa all over Russell and throwing her legs on him out of my head, but I was hoping to see him. So I figured if I stayed over Cookie's long enough, I could spot him going home. As I made it to the corner of her house, I saw Mrs. Corine (their mom, may she RIP) coming out of their building's entrance.

"They ain't home," she informed me. "They went to All People's."

All Peoples is a community center that we kids all went to growing up. It is still a thriving center that does great events and services for the kids. Disappointed, I just bid her goodbye salutations and headed back to the street light and waited to cross. I crossed Maple Street and passed Mama Stella's house and waved to her sitting on the porch. She wasn't sitting there when I first come that way, and I just lackadaisically went about my way. Russell was coming out of the field where the big, old, pink house once stood. People had made a walking path through the field from years and years of crossing through it, making a shortcut. It seemed as though butterflies entered my body and were dancing to their own tune in my stomach. I wanted to cover my face and run, but he had gotten too close to me. I didn't know what to do or say, but he did. He said, "So if it isn't my little secret admirer."

I felt as though I would die right then and there. I stopped walking and smiled. I was embarrassed, and he kept talking. "How old are you?" he asked me.

I couldn't lie because I looked every bit of my age, so I told the truth. "Thirteen," I answered, matter of fact.

"Do you know how old I am?" he asked me.

I told him that I didn't, and he gave me the answer, "I am twenty-six years old. In September, I will be twenty-seven. Your folks would kill me if they even thought I was messing with you." He continued, "But I got all your letters at home. They are actually sweet. In fact, I got one in my wallet. Did someone help you write them?"

I shook my head *no* as he kept talking, "But I am too old for you," and he Knick my face like a playful punch and was about to walk off.

And I blurted out, "Is Lisa your girlfriend!?"

He was walking away and made a sideward step to turn back in my direction and told me, "Nah, Lisa is crazy. She is just a friend. You jealous?" and he chuckled.

I turned away from him smiling and took off running. I felt as though he really probably thought I was crazy, but at least he knew that *I* wanted to be his girlfriend.

There were two girls who used to walk up and down the streets on Maple, going back and forth to the liquor store. They were what we called *high yellow*. They had long, *good hair* and looked like they were of Mexican descent. They hung around Mexicans, but they looked mixed. There was no bi-racial back then that I knew of, either you were black, Mexican, white Chinese, or mixed. I later found out they were Russell's cousins. They were Creole too. We used to talk about them girls, and I even attempted to fight the youngest one named Virginia because she always tried to be bad. Once I found out she was Russell's cousin, I changed my attitude toward her. I talked to Russell more now that he knew I liked him and felt he had set me straight about him being too old for me. I told him about his *stuck-up* cousins too.

One day, he was sitting on our porch just chilling. He thought it was funny. He told me that they were really nice girls if I would get to know them; but in my mind, I doubted if they would ever like me after all the names I had called them. But the oldest girl Carmelita was cooler than Virginia. I liked Carmelita. After all, I thought one day, they would be my family too.

I was not hurt that Russell thought I was too young for him, but I did channel my energies back to fighting the neighborhood boys, climbing trees, and playing in the park. I still saw Russell from time to time, getting off work or going to the bookie joint or just hanging out sitting on the grass in the park. Wall Street was a busy little street, and it was always something going on day and night. Russell never became my husband, but he sure did bail me out of hot water when I felt I had no one else in the world who could. It wasn't until I was older that I realized Russell was my Ram in the bush, and God placed him in my path to serve that purpose and that purpose only. What Russell did for me could have cost him his life. He became my baby's father. I tried to live a normal life, but it is very hard to do so when you are being molested.

I was surfing the internet and found a page called Wikipedia and put sexual abuse in the search engine. There was a plethora of information on sexual abuse, but I wasn't looking for it to write an essay. I just wanted to read up on it, and what I found was this: Fifteen to twenty-five percent of women were sexually abused when they were children. Thirty percent are relatives, sixty percent are acquaintances, and ten percent are strangers. I fell into all the categories. I used to believe I was a *walking vagina* or had a stamp on my head that read, "your turn." That is why I could identify with Oprah Winfrey's character, Sophia, in the movie *the Color Purple* when she said, "All my life, I had to fight…"

If I weren't being chased by men pulling up in their cars playing with themselves, I was being chased by older boys trying to touch my private parts. When I spend the night over friend's houses, their brothers would try to grind on me; and sometimes, the girls themselves would do *things* to me. I was a magnet for sexual predators like honey is for bees. I know kids, and I have done it myself, play house and kissing games and what have you; but that's kids playing. But when grown men think it is okay to take young girls or boy's virginity that is not kosher at all.

I was sexually abused, and I became pregnant. I knew in my heart I could never tell who I was pregnant by because I really didn't know. I was being molested at home and by a neighbor. I couldn't blame one or the other, so I fabricated stories. I said I was raped (which wasn't far from the truth) by a man coming from school. Then I changed the story every time someone would ask me, even my god-sitter Ruby, who I loved dearly, tried to get it out of me. I lied to her too. I just couldn't tell the truth. Something in me kept telling me I would mess up everyone's life, and I would be sent away; and that I would have to have an abortion, and I would never see my family again. So I hid my pregnancy under big clothes. The funny thing is that—as I look back on all of this—no one ever seen me go anywhere but home, school, and church; and occasionally, over some friends' houses. So why they couldn't or wouldn't put two and two together behooved me. Then I surmised they knew but didn't want to face the fact that they allowed me to fall through the cracks. So in April of 1972, some lucky sperm from one of my abusers impregnated me; and I hid it for almost four months. I went to school in big clothes, didn't want to socialize much anymore, and felt embarrassed to hang around my friends for fear they would find out and tease me. So I bowed out of my circle of comfort and waited for whatever was going to happen.

Russell had not come around as much as he'd once had, and I became focused on trying to continue my education. I went to a pregnant girl's school once it all came out that I was pregnant; and I swole up overnight it seems. It seems as though once the truth came out that I was pregnant, I was big as a house. It surprised a lot of people that the tomboy of the hood was pregnant, but it wasn't as bad as I thought it would be. No one hated me or called me names. They actually got over the shock and treated me the same. In fact, I was still trying to climb trees; and my dad caught me one day as he had come home from work and yelled at me, "Get yo' ass outta that damn tree!" The folks who were on the porch laughed.

Ava and I used to make cookies and candies and sell them to people who came to sit on the porch. No one would eat our goodies except for Uncle Red. Uncle Jeff would sometimes, but he and my dad talked about how the cookies looked bad. By this time, Uncle Red knew I had liked Russell; and I asked him to give Russell a note for me. When I couldn't find Uncle Red, I would ask Russell's cousin, Steven, to take it to him. To keep people from knowing, I would put it in a brown paper bag as though I was given Steven something to eat. Steven was a big dude, and so it all worked out. Everyone was still trying to figure out who my baby daddy was, and I didn't know what I was going to do, but I was looking for my ram in the bush. I don't know to this day if God was leading me, or I was just intelligent enough to figure this all out on my own. I do not believe it was the latter.

One day, the walls were closing in on me; and I was sitting on my porch. And as custom was for most folks who worked and knew about Wall Street, they came to drink, play dominoes, or just *shoot the breeze* before they went home. This day, Russell stayed longer than usual; and I was embarrassed to see him 'cause I was pregnant and didn't know if he had heard. When the people began to trickle away, as it was getting late, Russell made his way over to where I sat and told me, "Stevie gave me my lunch."

He was referring to the letter I had given his cousin Steven to give to him. Normally, I was pledging my undying love to him; but in the letter he was referring to, I just asked if I could talk to him. I cannot remember verbatim what I wrote, but this is basically what it pertained to: "Russell, I need to talk to you. I know you probably heard I was pregnant, and everybody trying to figure out who the father is. I told them I was raped to keep them off my back, but later I recanted that story when I came up with a plan. I know I'm younger than you, but I don't want my baby to not have a daddy. I want my baby to have a daddy he can look up too."

And I told him the truth who had molested me because I felt he needed to know the truth. Believe me. I myself don't know where all this came from. I was thirteen, going on fourteen, and I concluded, "You don't have to love me, and I won't be jealous if you have other girlfriends your age. I just want to use your name," and that was the premise of my letter. I remember it well because I never forgot that day.

I must have sounded really crazy to Russell because it all sounded crazy to me, but it was as though I had left my body and someone else had taken over. And Russell looked at me in disbelief, not about what I had asked him but because of who had been molesting me and said, "That mutha———a," and he hugged me right there on the porch. Just I and he, as mostly everyone was gone and looked at me and said, "Tell them I am the baby daddy."

My love and respect for Russell was even greater. Here I was thinking all this time I had that little school-girl crush on him that would fade and go away, but God had set it in motion so that my child would not have to be raised up in shame and vain, being teased about his daddy. My baby was born healthy and strong, I didn't care about how he was conceived, he was mine, now ours, and that was all that mattered. And Russell was with me every step of the way, every pain and groan.

After a few heads turned and wigs were blown back, the novelty of me and Russell being together wore off. There was never really much said about the whole situation, which is sad in and of itself because once they found out Russell was the daddy and I wasn't raped by the football team, the grittiness of the story wasn't as good to gossip about. Russell made a grand sacrifice for us. My mother was puzzled, and I think she had her suspicions that he wasn't my son's dad, but she let it alone. Russell and I never actually laid together as man and wife because I was pregnant and underage, but he lived with us and took care of us and stayed between his grandmother's Mau-Mau's house and ours. Moses would even come and check on us and buy anything we needed as well. I think they all knew once he was born. My baby was *light skinned,* but that was all he could have gotten from Russell, but he was ours.

As I grew older, I wished I had stayed with Russell and had babies by him; but as I mentioned previously, I wasn't steering this ship. When our son turned six-month-old, a voice told me that I had to leave Russell so he could go on with his life; but when I told him that, he was so upset and heartbroken. He didn't understand it, and I couldn't explain it then. I just know I heard that voice, and it had to be. I believe now that God had a plan for us to meet to save each other. Naturally, in those six months, I really fell in love with him; and I think he had grown emotionally attached to me, acting like a child at times and all, but he never left my side. When the day came for us to separate, he was distraught. We had just bought a 1955 Ford from our neighbors who had brought it from Mexico and wanted to sell it. I couldn't drive it, so I told Russell about it, and he bought it for $100. And it would be that very car that would drive us out of his life. The night before he was to take us to Blythe because I felt that moving to Blythe would be the best for us and him to go on with his life, he asked me to do one thing for him, "Lena, promise me you will never give my son another father or another name." And to this day, many have tried; but I never changed my son's name.

I can't remember if that car was a Ford or a Chevy, but I remember it was a '55. I loved that car, and I sure wish I could have driven it. I would probably still have it. I love old cars still. The day we loaded up the car, My Uncle Chico (RIP) rode along with us so Russell wouldn't be alone, plus Uncle Chico loved my Big Mama; and any chance he would get to go see her he would. Russell was very quiet on the ride to Blythe. I know he was hurting. I was too, but that voice was adamant in me to let this man go. I don't know what God had planned for Russell, but I felt compelled to be obedient. I got out of the car, and he held his son and me for a very long time and had tears in his eyes; and I was crying, and he kept telling me *I didn't have to go through with this. That everything would turn out okay.*

But the only thing that came out my mouth was, "You did it for me. Now I have to do this for you." And he kissed us both; and after my uncle Chico went in to hug Big Mama, then my family all came out to say good bye. They got in the car and left us standing on the sidewalk waving.

At the time of this writing, my baby was thirty-six years old. Now he is forty-four. He met Russell over the years a few times and still carries his name, and his kids carry his name. I have searched for him every time I go to Los Angeles and throughout Louisiana. I have not found him yet; but if he is alive, I pray to God just like he brought us together so many years ago. I pray that he will find it in his will to let us see each other again, just so he can see his grandkids; and I can tell him one more time just how much I love him. I just want him to know that I felt I did this for him so he could have a life without anyone looking down on him and calling him a cradle robber and just demeaning him. I didn't think of all the child support that would follow him for the rest of his life burdening him, or the fact that this may cause a hindrance in his livelihood; but I never heard anything. And I believe I never did because God was leading me in all of it. I do know this though. I think Russell was one hell of a man to do what he did for me, and that's why I could not write a book without including him in it, to publicly acknowledge him for his dedication to us. Wherever he is, I just hope his family knows just what kind of a man he was, and I hope still is.

And if you never have another child, you will always have ours. Your name lives on through him. *We found Russell through his daughter on FB in Louisiana and unfortunately we didn't get a chance to reunite with him before his passing August 17, 2020. Respect.

Watermelon Tramp

(To Doe Doe)

It was hot and the sun was beaming on an ant that crawled in the dirt before me as I watched it desperately trying to get over the rocks in its path. I drifted into a daydream to a time in my life when I was that ant desperately struggling to get over the rocks of my life. I had placed myself in a field, a time that held memories dear to my heart and the men who lived there with me. *The Watermelon Tramps*, who were my life, a part of my home.

I was coming out of the Flamingo, a club in Blythe California, owned by Mr. Otis Parrish and his brother Murt. It was the local club for anyone to go to, but mostly blacks frequented it. The club had been a part of the black community since before I was born in 1958. The *Flamingo*, affectionately called the *Mango* was a beer and wine joint that took pride is playing its music on a *juke-box*. Some of the music on there was as old as I was, and we had to make sure that Mr. Otis or Mr. Murt would change it from time to time. The only reason why I thought that I had carte blanche was because Mr. Otis and my mother had been dating since before I was born. For a long time, I didn't know that he was married and looked at him as a father figure. In fact, on numerous occasions, I heard old folk say he was my daddy.

I was in town that day, and it was anywhere from 110 to 120 degrees under the shade, and at night having such weather would not be a surprise. But I had on some Eskimo boots that were really stylish. I had not been long coming from the *City of Angels*, Los Angeles,

71

so I still was dressing as though I was a city girl. I had on a pair of shorts, a halter top, and my boots. I was Lena. I ran my show, and I didn't care who liked it or what they said about it 'cause I always believed that *I* was the *princess of Blythe*. I practically knew everyone. I got whatever I wanted, and I felt all the boys and men wanted to get *at* me, so I figured, wasn't that princess' criteria? I was a spoiled brat in my own world, but I was not obnoxious. I just knew how to work my *gifts*. My brother Charlie used to always tell me I was moving too fast for Blythe.

As I was crossing the street to go home, I heard someone say, "Damn who is that?" and I kept walking but was silently gloating that I was attracting attention.

Then I heard someone say, "I heard she have crabs."

My heart skipped five beats, and that gloating turn into embarrassment and shame. I almost stopped in my tracks to cuss out whoever had said that, but I was supposed to be profiling, so I just trotted off into a sensuous gait to my grandmother's house. My Big Mama's house was not that far from the Mango. She lived on Rice, and the Flamingo was on Second Street, and the two streets intersected. She was on the right of intersection; and the club was on the left, twenty yards apart, if that much. But after hearing that remark, seem as though it took me forever to make it to that gate; and it seem that everyone and their ancestors heard it. I was mad and hurt. I was going to see if Robbie and Sheila were home, who lived next door; but my mind wasn't on that then.

I had gone to get a beer out of the Flamingo and some money from my mother (not the beer from her though, I had to get someone to sneak one out to me), and it was then that I heard that voice screaming that out into the night air, or so it had seemed he screamed it. I sat in the yard, and a feeling of doomed just hit me. Then I thought about the time I went over to visit Robbie, and Sheila was home, and everyone was sitting on the bed. But when I walked in to sit, she hurriedly said, "Oh, here, Lena. Sit over here," and she put a towel on the bed; and the other girls who were over there stopped what they were doing and looked up from the magazine they were all trying to look through.

Robbie spoke up and said, "Sheila, you don't have to do that." Then Robbie looked at me and said, "Here, Lena, you can sit here," and she moved some clothes from her bed; and I sat down. I didn't know it then; but later on, I figured out that Shelia had heard the same ugly rumor. But instead of them telling me, they just left me in the dark. Sheila was *funny* like that anyway, so I didn't take it to heart. I had seen her treat other people with her funny ways before.

While my mind was playing tricks on me as I sat there in the dark, smoking my cigarettes and sipping on my beer, I was trying to figure out how that rumor got started. The night was starting off so well. It was watermelon season, and all the watermelon tramps were coming into town, and I didn't want to miss that because I knew whenever anyone came to town—harvest time or not—the Flamingo was the place to stop and browse in. That night was the browsing night. One thing about harvest time was that men and women alike knew that the harvest was ripe, and I am not talking about the vegetables and fruits. I am talking about the men and women who came out to see what they could find. It was almost a tradition that if you went through the whole year without a man or woman, you could get one during watermelon season; and if your boyfriend was acting a fool before the season, you surely could pay him back by making him jealous during melons time. The men came from miles around: New York, Chicago, Detroit, Arizona (Eloy and Casa Grande), Indio, California, Banning California, Bakersfield, California, Delano California, El Centro, Brawley, and so many other places in between. It was a potpourri of men. Talk about a variety of fruit! And trust me, they left their seeds too. To this day, their seeds are still growing with seeds of their own.

The watermelon business was a big business. As I mentioned before, I was born in 1958; and watermelons were being planted and harvested before then. Nish Farms, Fisher Farms, and Arkalian farms were three of the main *fruit and vegetable* farms in Blythe. Mr. Nish and Mr. Fisher were white, and Mr. Arkalian was Armenian. The only importance about that is that there were also black businessmen who had the vehicles to transport the crops from the fields. Bob Erath and his brother, Bennie Brookins, were some of the truckers who had a fleet of watermelon trucks to go into the fields go get loaded; and they would get crews together to *swamp* the trucks. Meaning, they picked the fruit up out of the fields once another crew had cut the vines the fruit was on. At the end of the day, the workers could get a *teeta*. That is an advancement on their paychecks. Some of them would teeta out their whole checks, and that is what kind of an evening it was that night. People had gotten their teetas, and it was time to party.

I went back to the club after pondering the thought, and I went back with my head held high as though I hadn't heard anything. I stepped into my groove, and everything else faded into the night. All the fun was outside the Flamingo anyway because the majority of us were too young to go inside; so we all partied outside with music blasting from car stereos, jamming to eight-track tapes. I creeped inside while the dance floor was packed and met the love of my life (I thought), and it was Walter Betters. He was out of Eloy, and his homeboys called him *Doe Doe*. Now I was thinking Doe Doe meant *money*. I could not have been further from the truth. He sat in a corner and kept his eye on me and stood up and walked over to me and asked me to dance. He was at least six two and built. I didn't know if them melons were his weights or what, but I could tell through that nylon T-shirt he had on that he had *guns* (muscles). He was chocolate and had an afro that looked like one of the Sylvers. He was a fine specimen of a man. He towered me and was looking down at me gritting his teeth, and it looked as though he was grinning then not grinning, and I didn't know whether to be infatuated or run.

When he asked me my name, he tilted his head to one side, a trademark of his; and before I could answer, he had my hands in his and was pulling me to the dance floor. It was getting late, so Mr. Otis didn't mind us coming in to dance. After we danced, I thanked him and was about to walk away when he grabbed me and asked, "So where your man at?"

I turned to him, and I said, "He at home in bed," and I paused and declared, "and he's one years old," and I walked away. He just stood there, gritting his teeth, making that face grinning and not grinning. No, Doe Doe did not mean money. I was sure it meant *nut*, but I smiled at the thought of him looking at me like that.

I had been in Blythe a year, and I had been running around with Shorty Armstrong, Joe Armstrong, and Daylee Sauls. Shorty and I was liking each other, and I would spend a lot of time with them just hanging out, going on Bell Lane where they lived and chilling. But when I wasn't with them, I would be with Robbie or just by myself. There was another watermelon tramp in town that caught my eyes. His name was Ernest Wright. He was thick. A big gargantuan type thickness, fine as heck from Oklahoma. I had met him before I met Doe Doe; but this summer, I was interested in them both. But Doe Doe ended up sweeping me off my feet, literally took me from Shorty, Ernest, and whoever else might have been interested. He made sure he nipped that in the bud.

One day, Ernest had come to see me after he had come out of the fields and asked me to come by his place later. He lived at the El Solano Motel with his brothers Elbert, James, and Nate, and one of their homeboys Trash (yep, they called him Trash). I told him that I would, and he left. That evening, Robbie, Sheila, and I all walked down to the motel which was only a block away on Spring Street. When we got there, Virgie Austin was their too. Sheila and Robbie were known as the De Loach girls to the watermelon men because their dad Uncle Red was a cutter, and he also had a few trucks or drove them. Their fellows knew who their daddy was, so no one messed with them. They were treated with respect. We were all having fun. Trash was being silly as he always were, and Ernest and I was lying across his bed. In reality, it was whoever bed got it for the night, and I remember daydreaming, thinking of what life would be like with him. He was so cute and quiet and so good looking, down home kind of guy; and he loved playing with my son when he came around. I thought of how moving to Oklahoma to be with him would be so wonderful—then Walter popped in my head. He changed all that thinking.

Walter showed up on the sidewalk in front of my Big Mama's house for the next three years. He continued to come through, and I followed after him as he followed the harvest. I would visit him at the motels he lived in or the kitchenettes he rented with another tramp. I went through summers and off seasons with him, loving him and waiting for him to return. When he wasn't around, I talked to other men. He had another family, and I knew he was not a saint. I didn't ever think of us as husband and wife or saw it in the future; but when we were together, we were together, and I loved it and loved him. There were some in Blythe who could live like that; but for me, I wanted something more, but I didn't know that until all that changed in Banning California. It changed for me when I went to live with Walter at the Edge Motel on the outskirts of Banning on Ramsey. He had women clothes in the room in his dresser which was supposed to be our room, and we fought the whole time I was there. His excuse was so lame I can't even remember it, but I was done. His home-boy Robert Scott—we called him CC (chocolate city) and the girl he was with, Althea—knew because when I brought it up, they didn't say anything. Never once did they try to intercede to say I was wrong or right, so that made me believe I was right, and I felt it was time for me to go. Once before, I had come there; and my Uncle Dick Hammond brought me back home to Blythe with him. He wasn't there that time, but I knew I was going to leave.

Dwayne McKaney, he was from Casa Grande Arizona, had stopped by the motel to take Walter to Indio, California. I told Walter to tell him to drop me off on his way to Blythe because I was going to get on the greyhound, and it didn't make sense to do that, and they were going in my direction. I was not that mad. So once Doe was ready, I had already packed my suitcase. We all took off. It was a forty-five-minute ride from Banning to Indio, and an hour and a half from Indio to Blythe. Walter and I rode in silence. He and Dwayne made small talk, but the music sent us all into our own little worlds. When we came into Indio from the back road, off Jefferson, we took Doe to the club on the outskirts of Indio where his mother, Mrs. Mary, was the manager. He open the door and held it so I could get out and get into the front seat, and he stopped me before I could slide in.

The watermelon tramps legacy in Blythe was an awesome part of the history of that little town. Then crack came along and gang-banging, and politics and Blythe just have never been the same. Many fared well. Many didn't, but it wasn't the fault of the fruit. It was all of our faults, giving into and out of open love; and secret lovers and relationships gone wrong. Some who had found love from this era are still together. Some are gone on to glory, young and old. I loved the watermelon season, and I love Blythe still. Some people are still living off the wealth that the harvest brought them, and some have squandered the money and years of hard work that went into fields and driving and swamping that gave so many a way of life. I was the princess of the fields. I could go where no other girls could or were allowed to because of who I was. I had been riding in watermelon trucks, going into the fields and the sheds since I was in my mother's womb. My mother was the *queen of Blythe* to me. She knew everyone, and everyone loved her and respected her. She was wanted by many, but only chose a few. Until the day she died in 2008, people only had good things to say about her.

I was her legacy. I carried on for her. I was self-proclaimed, but I was valid. My grandfather, father (s) and uncles, cousins, brothers, and friends were all involved in the melons somehow. My Big Mama always had a house full, feeding people, giving them a place to sleep (even if only on the floor). She turned down no one and tried to feed every one. Some paid. Some couldn't, but they always came back. There are not many in the black community who can say that they didn't have the love of my grandma. And I took it all in, and it evolved in me as I grew up. I mentioned fathers because it was always a joke in our family that I had four daddies: R. D. Rogers, Otis Parrish, Jessie Hammond, and Chester Whitney. My birth certificate says Rogers, but Uncle Dick said I am a Hammond and don't ever think that I am not. I loved all four of them, and they are all gone, but they all treated me as though I was theirs. They all played important roles in my life. I write this book for them.

I remember when I found out why I was rumored to have crabs back then. It was a cruel thing that someone in my family had sex with someone, and we exchanged clothes regularly; and doing one of those exchanges, I had worn some of her clothes, and she knew she had them and didn't tell me. No one ever came to me personally to tell me I had crabs, but one person; and I was very embarrassed about that for a while. Later, I found that it was Walter who had asked about me that night when I was in my fancy boots walking to my grandmother's house and had it not been for me over hearing his conversation with someone that rumor would have floated around for a while. By the time, I had gone to the clinic, the doctor said I didn't have anything, and it could have been an isolated case of the mite being carried in the clothes. Needless to say, I learned a valuable lesson to not wear other people's clothing or trusting the clothes to be cleaned.

When I made it back home, when Dwayne dropped me off, I was so glad to be home, so glad to be alive. I will never forget that day because the last thing Walter said to me is, "You still gonna write that book?"

I had always told him that I would write a book about the watermelon tramps, and I looked at him and said, "Yes." And for my Doe Doe, my nut (I know that sounds nasty but Walter was nutty when he wanted to be), and my Sweet Pea of Sacramento, I wrote this. Walter put his hand on my chin and lifted my lips toward his and kissed them and said, "Bye."

And almost inaudibly, I whispered, "Bye."

Then he said, to me, "I'll always love you, girl," and he walked away; and I watched him entered the little juke joint and walk out of my life. I couldn't even tell him that I would always love him. The emotions in me were in my throat. Teary eyed, I got in the front seat of Dwayne's white classic Lincoln, and *we got on.*

Later in life, I found out that Doe had a baby, by my god-sister Margaret. I only smiled. I said to myself, *well, at least he kept it in the family.* I didn't see Walter for many years after that day; and when I learned he was clean and sober and living a good productive life, I was amazed and so very proud of him. We are in contact again, and he is doing great. The way he lived, everyone thought he would be amongst the ones who have gone on to glory; but watermelon heaven ain't ready for him yet.

As Dwayne and I cross that vast desert heading on to Blythe, we made small talk and listened to his eight track playing them good oldies; and we just rolled along, watching the road, watching the sands of the desert pass us by. When we finally made it to Blythe, I sighed. As he had come to a stop in front of my grandma's house on Rice Street, and I was getting out of his car, my son ran out the door so excited to see me. He cried out, "Mama!" And I knew I was home, where *I needed to be*.

Ode to Yolanda Washington

(Killed by the Hillside Strangler)

I had finally arrived at Junior High School, and I was excited about it. It was 1970, and it promised to be the best time of my life. I was in Student Achievement Classes (SAC) because I was an over achiever and did well in school and was considered one of the elite students. When they first told me I was going to be in *special* classes, I was against it. I thought they were trying to put me in special education for the slow students; but once they explained it to me, I was happy about it. The teachers from my elementary school had labeled me as bright and having great potential to succeed; so despite the hell I gave them at San Pedro Elementary school, I was recommended for the SAC classes at John Adams Junior High School.

In my first year, actually the first week, I had an array of friends, new and old ones. Some of the girls and boys I had graduated sixth grade with didn't make it to SAC, so I didn't see them as much in classes; and when it was lunch time, they had begun to hang in clicks. I was edged out of their circles, either from jealousy; or they just felt I was no longer their cup of tea. It didn't bother me much because I met new friends. In fact, Georgette Hudson was one *new friend* who taught me a valuable lesson about friendship. We became close, and we laughed and played in class, did our homework and school projects together, and talked about boys. She was a pretty girl. She was bright-skinned and wore long puffy ponytails and had a big smile. I remember telling her that I like this one boy in class named Prince (his real name). Prince would come to our table and make us laugh, and he would always flirt with me and said that he liked me. Well, one day, I gave Georgette a letter to give to him, telling him I like him too; and I would be his girlfriend. A few of the other kids by now knew that I liked Prince and that he supposedly liked me, and he and I and Georgette were a trio. I was out of school for a few days, I think I had went to Blythe California to visit my grandmother because she was sick. When I came back, Georgette and Prince were boyfriend and girlfriend; and our little trio had dwindle to those two. The kids in our class made fun of me when I returned, laughing at me because I had thought Georgette was my friend. I don't recall who it was, but a girl walked by me and she said, "Bet you won't be giving nobody else letters to give to your boyfriend." The girl was being mean-spirited, but she was absolutely right. I had learned a valuable lesson that stayed with me to my adult years.

Remember, I said going to Junior High had promised to be the best time of my life? I was so wrong. I met another *new friend* who I thought was really cool with me. Her name was Marshall (pronounced Mar-Shell) Allen. She was a homely looking girl, but she was alright. She acted like a little old lady and laughed loudly and shook her hair when she laughed. She had a nice grade of hair and wore it like a curly natural most of the time. She was what my mother would call an old soul. Well, that old soul had a hidden mean streak in her; and I had to find that out in the most embarrassing way. Marshall stopped hanging around me and started walking around school with some other girls. She never came to me and said why she just stopped being *my friend*. I noticed that a few people would look at me funny when I walked by, and some would snicker at me and point. I didn't know what had happened.

My mother had not really prepared me for being on my menstrual cycle, and I forgot all about what they taught us in health classes. I was a tomboy. I didn't think about that sort of thing even happening to me. The movie *Carrie* (11-23-76) hadn't come out yet, so I didn't know they all were *going to laugh at me*. So when I started my cycle, I didn't take a bath that day because I had heard girls weren't supposed to take a bath on their cycle; or they would cramp to death. In fact, I didn't let my mother know I had begun my menstruation, and other kids had said using toilet paper and napkins was just as good. So I unbeknownst to me, I got a reputation for not smelling too fresh.

When we completed our SAC classes for the day in the bungalows designated for SAC students, the remainder of our classes were in the Administration Building near the building that was also the cafeteria and the student book store. My classes were in the Administration Building. After the bell had rung, and we were let out, Marshall and a group of girls passed by me laughing and holding on to one another as though what they were whispering was so funny; and they went ahead of me. Now the boys who might have heard that I didn't smell so good didn't treat me any different. They still talked to me, but those girls had been very awful toward me. As I was going up the stairs to go to my class on the second floor, out of nowhere, Marshall and her friends walked behind me and started chanting, "Fish! Fish! Fish!" And they'd run by me again as though if they were to touch me they would turn into fish as well. Then it dawned on me they were saying I stank. Fish stinks, and they were calling me fish; so they had to be going around telling people I stank. I continued on up the stairs, feeling bad, mad, and embarrassed and hurt. I went to my class and endured them.

After the class was over, we all had to go to the Physical Education building to prepare for gym class. Once the bell rung and we kids were let out, I walked amongst the crowd as students ran in all directions trying to beat the next bell to their respective classes. As I was going down the stairs, again, Marshall and her little entourage ran by me calling me names. I didn't hear what I was being call that time because I had made up my mind. She would never call me fish again.

Marshall's locker was two lockers from mine, and she was standing there alone and not saying anything to me. So I started the conversation, "Marshall, why you keep calling me names?" and before she could get any words out of her mouth, I had walked over there to her and pushed her. She tumbled on the floor, and I screamed at her, "Where are your friends now? Do something now!" I continued as I went to straddle her as she tried to get off the floor. Then I heard,

"Fight! Fight, fight, fight!" And she scrambled to get off the floor, and I had a lock of *her laughing afro*, and we were swinging! I tried to tear her ass up. Embarrassing me like that, and she was supposed to be my friend.

Suddenly, Ms. Jones, the black gym teacher, was standing in between us and had come to break up the fight. The two of us were heaving and breathing hard, and I looked at Marshall, and all I could say was, "I might smell like a fish but I don't fight like one!" and I heard some of the older girls laugh at my outburst; but I didn't care then. I had redeemed myself.

Ms. Jones (I don't know if she was married or not) took us to the office and made us explain what the fight was all about. Still yelling, I told her about the name calling and how they were treating me; and as she spoke to us, I heard sympathy in her voice for me. She sent Marshall to the principal's office and kept me for a few minutes longer to give me some hygiene tips. As I sat there seething and listening to her but not listening to her, I had already put it in my mind that no one would ever smell me again or be able to talk about me like that again in my life. Marshall and I never were friends again; and when her mother came to the school to speak with the principal about me, I could see why Marshall was so loud and old fashion herself. She actually tried to yell at me for beating her daughter up; and I yelled back at her, telling her that her daughter should not have been so mean to me. I didn't tell my mother about the fight for a day. The school finally called and told her I was suspended, and then she took me up there to get me back in school. I thought I was going to get a whooping, but she sat me down and talked to me about the whole thing. I was relieved. I really liked Marshall. I thought she was a funny girl. I think I was more hurt by her actions than anything. I know now that if she had been a true friend, she would have told *me* I smelled and not spread it all over school like that. I didn't really ever hear that from anyone but that group of girls, but I felt as though the whole school knew and I felt isolated and withdrawn, but *nobody* messed with me or talked about me again, not in my face.

In hindsight, I can say that there really was no excuse for me not having better hygiene about myself; but I was a young girl who lived with an alcoholic mother and a dad who looked at me in ways a father shouldn't and being molested by a man who I thought was a *friend of the family*. I had a lot on my plate to be so young. That fishy smell they smelled was probably a mixture of my flow and semen and dirt all together. I wasn't taking douches at twelve or thirteen years old. I was just trying to enjoy being a kid. I spent the better part of my seventh grade running on sidewalks and hiding in between cubby holes, trying to escape from my abuser who stalked me as though I was his prey; and in a way, I was. I was so afraid on a daily basis that he would get me or find me that I sometimes didn't want to go home. I didn't even like taking baths at home because sometimes I would look up, and he would be peeking in the bathroom at me. He knew when I would be home alone. I dropped so many hints to my family, but no one picked up on them. And once when I tried to tell my mother, when he caught me alone, he showed me a gun and said if I told anyone, anytime, he would killed my whole family. He threatened me with acid too. It could have been water. I didn't try to see. He even stalked me when I went to school, parking along the streets, watching me, trying to make sure I didn't talk to any boys or walk home with any boys. No matter which way I turned he was lurking.

Every moment at school was a reprieve though. I dreaded going home, and I dreaded being in the hood now. Sometimes I just wanted to run away (and one time I did, and *he* came looking for me). I was afraid because there were so many abductions during this time. The world to me was fast becoming an ugly place to be in. I wanted to kill myself. School was all I had, and that safe haven was taken from me too; he was stalking me, and my circle of friends that I could talk to or confide in, had become few to none. I felt so alone; and looking back, that is when I realized that life was in session. I stopped being a child at age eleven and became a mother at age fourteen. The only good in my life at that time was bringing my son into this ugly world. Somehow, I knew that he would be my ticket out of the madness that had engulfed my life. All I ever wanted was to be a kid, enjoy my life, grow up to marry one of my many homeboys I had a crush on, and live life happily ever after. That was just a vision that went in the trash along with my baby's dirty diapers.

I transferred from John Adams, and enrolled in Edison Junior High School near Gage and Compton Ave, in 1972. I did that because I had found out I was pregnant and didn't want to go through any more embarrassing phases at Adam's again, so I went to be with Ava at Edison. She was and still is my real true friend who never judged me and was always there for me. She had left living in the twenties long before I did, but we always kept in touch some kind of way; and when she asked her parents if I could use their address to go to Edison, we both were thrilled when they said I could. One day, I had woke up and all the abuse stopped just as abruptly as it had started. I think being pregnant scared them off, but it was too late then. I had become a little woman. My life was my own, and it was my son's. I ended up leaving L.A. altogether. After I went to Edison, I left there and went to a girl's pregnant school on Avalon near Avalon Park. I never had the opportunity to graduate from junior high school, and I really missed that I didn't get to finish school with my friends (and I say that loosely) and classmates and join in the festivities of being a student. Attending junior high school looked promising, but no one told me it would be, what did I know? I was a silly little girl, with silly little dreams. I still played cowboys and Indians.

I left L.A. and moved to my hometown Blythe and lived there until I left in my senior year of high school. School just didn't seem to do it for me. I moved to Oakland California, three months before I was to graduate. I just did as the song says, "Hop on the bus Gus. No need to discuss much, just drop off the key, lee, and get yourself free…"

I went through a bad relationship, and I did just that. I stayed in Oakland from 1976 to 1977, leaving behind another long list of crazy men and so-called friends. It was in 1977 that I became re-acquainted with an old John Adam's student whom I thought was really nice. Only I wouldn't be meeting her face to face no time soon because she had been killed, and I would be reading about her in a newspaper.

I enrolled in Los Angeles Trade Technical College as soon as I returned to LA. I had tried to go to school in Oakland, but I had a run in with another man who insisted on stalking me, so I came

85

home. I was determined to get an education, but I had the darndest time fulfilling that dream. I didn't always read the newspaper either; but on the college campus, it seemed to be the *in thing*. It was a scary time back then. Young girls were being murdered and found in various places in the Los Angeles County areas by someone called the Hillside Strangler (Hillside Strangler Murders). I had heard about them, but I didn't let it get to me because I felt that what would happen, would happen. If it was meant to be, it would be. I had too much to worry about day by day. I could not afford to stress about the potential of other crimes being committed toward me. I was trying to get over having been mentally and physically abused in Oakland. I had spent the better part of my year in Oakland fighting men and women who thought I was easy game because I was new to town and trying to make a living for me and my son. I was so mentally burnt from abuse that my focus was not on anything but making a home for my child.

I was at Trade Tech talking to the campus police, and a few students in the K building where I worked in between classes when a young man holding the paper began talking about the murders. When he laid the paper down for us all to see the pictures of the girls who had been slain, I gasped when I saw Yolanda Washington's picture. I hadn't seen her in years, but I knew who she was immediately. One of the police officers there, Mr. Kennard who often visited the Information Center with Officer Shepherd to check on the late evening employees, asked me if I was okay when I gasped. I told him that I knew one of the girls and pointed to Yolanda. I read the details of the story and put the paper down. I just could not believe what I had read, but it was true in black and white print. The paper said that most of the girls that were killed were prostitutes; and that in the early investigation, they had thought Yolanda's boyfriend was her alleged pimp and that he may had killed her. She was later found to be the Hillside Strangler's first victim. It was so heartbreaking to read that she had been killed at all. Not one of them deserved to die in such a way, however, they chose to live their lives.

As I look back in my life and see and hear about various tragedies, I just thank God I was not in a predicament where I had to lose my life. I know anyone of those girls could have been me or someone in my family, given the area and time the murders all happened. Ever since the day, I read that paper and saw Yolanda's face in that picture. I never forgot it or her. I followed that case and always kept her in my heart and mind. I felt sorry for all the girls; but knowing one of my schoolmates died at the hands of those men changed my life and outlook on life. It made me reflect on the countless and careless times I had jumped in cars with strangers, taken drinks from strangers, and even gone home with strangers. When I lived in Oakland, I accepted a ride from a stranger after leaving a club in San Francisco; and we had to cross the Golden Gate Bridge. He could have killed me and dumped me in the bay. No one would have been the wiser. Not saying that these girls did any of those things, but it just made me come to terms with how little I valued myself and life.

When the Los Angeles police department realized that it was two men that were killing the women and not just one, they still called them the Hillside Strangler because the media had already played the name up in the media. These girls were snatched off sidewalks and dumped in rural areas and hillsides like they were not even human. Yolanda was the first one they killed. It was written and she was found near Forest Lawn Cemetery on October, 18, 1977. I came back to Los Angeles in the summer of 1977. She was still alive. I had just given my life to God and was baptized at a local church in South Central LA off Forty-Third and Avalon on McKinley. It was the Greater Mid-City Seventh-Day Adventist Church.

None of those girls deserved to die so viciously. I put the paper down, but the tears still filled my eyes. I didn't know Yolanda, and I can't say she was a friend; but I know when she saw me, she always gave me a big smile. I followed that story until they captured those killers in 1978. It took them fourteen years after the murders to convict them. It was said to have been one of the longest trials in the history of Los Angeles. Movies were made about them, and others that were made that were similar to the murders that weren't about them but just as gory. I still think of all of them, the victims and how they were murdered; and it is something that never leaves the back of my mind. I thank God on a daily basis for sparing my life and being in my life so many times when I had place my life in the devil's hands. I am not saying God didn't watch out for those women, but I have learned that we cannot question God for what he allows to happen and not happen. As I left work walking along the sidewalk in front of the college, headed to the bus stop, I couldn't get Yolanda's image out of my head. *How could she have died like that? If she was a prostitute or not, she was still a human being.*

I think of Yolanda a lot. I think of the times I saw her walking across the Adams campus being a hall monitor or dressed out in her gym clothes. I think about her smile and her walk, how she seemed to bounce when she walk. She was a good girl. She was a beautiful girl. She was a schoolmate and could have been a great friend.

Street Ventist

(Seventh-Day Street Ventist)

"In my Father's house are many mansions…" (John 14:2). That was supposed to have been my daily prayer to say every day before a meal. My Aunt Mandy gave it to me when I was three years old, but I could never say it right. I always said, "Down my Father's house are many main chins," and they thought it was the cutest thing. In retrospect, I now believe all that scripture really did was wet my appetite for the best, thinking my Father had many mansions and one was for me. I never really understood the gist of the scripture, but it made my Aunt Mandy and Uncle Herman smile, so I guess it made me happy too.

My cousin Charles' (may he rest in peace) prayer was *Jesus wept.* He was older, but he had the least words to learn, and now I wonder why? He'd had the shortest verse and the shorter life. Later on, he died at age eighteen. I had the longest verse and longer life of us too, and I would wonder if that played a part in it all, but I am always trying to analyze the past, present, and future incidents and therefore reasoned that, that's why I have come to believe this all led me to me being who I am today, a street Ventist.

I was born in a family of God-fearing women. I can't say that my family feared God because if they did, they wouldn't have partied like they did; but I'm only basing this on just recently experiencing the true meaning of fearing God. I believed my grandmother and her daughters, my mother and aunts, quite possibly had a fear of God because they believed in Him, knew He exist, and probably experienced some of His Powers; but not enough to stop drinking, cussing, and having relationships out of wedlock among other things. They weren't saintly, but they weren't a bad bunch neither. So what I'm saying is, individually, we all had to experience a relationship with God on our own to determine our own fear of God and His existence. I didn't understand what it meant to fear God until I was, well, into my forties; and even then, I didn't show a holy respect for the Master. So I cannot judge what my family feared or did not fear about God.

It is my own personal fear of God that I experienced that allows me to see this in hindsight. There are several examples of fear in scripture. "And when a person truly accepts the Lord God Jesus Christ as Savior and Lord, it is only through His teachings will fears be realized and conquered and believed upon, and no man can judge ones' fears." (See Psalms 112:1; 2 Timothy 1:7; Luke 23:40; and Philippians 4:7.)

I guess I inherited that same spiritualness from my family because I truly believed in God and truly asked God into my life and accepted Christ as my Personal Savior, but it didn't stop me from partying and being promiscuous and living adulterously. I had a fear for God, but it was subliminal. It was a twitching. It was the *I* in my sinful nature that craved that *need to live on the edge to know I was living* kind of fear, and boy did I live on the edge. Despite all my physical and mental challenges that kept me in an out of church, I had a need within me to be there. I was in my forties when I came to realize that living on the edge does not a Christian make. It only puts me closer to dying without the true knowledge of God's love and His purpose for my life as His child; and deep, deep, deep in my heart, I always felt that I was a child of God. Sister Casoli made sure I knew that. My family did their best to instill that feeling in me, and God himself gave me the desire or will in my heart by placing people, places, and things in my life to get the message to me.

I left Blythe in my senior year and moved to Oakland, California with the clothes on my back and a three-year-old son and a hand full of brand new clothes I had stolen out of stores throughout Blythe and a welfare check. I remember sitting in the Oakland bus station wondering, *what had I done?* I walked outside to the sidewalk and looked around (not believing I'd really made it) and decided to try to call my cousin Robbie (who I hadn't been able to reach) and finally catching her on the phone. She told me she had no way to come get me; so I caught a cab, not realizing it would take all my little change. We had talked about me coming to live out there but not that day. After reaching her, I dropped all my brand new clothes in the nearest trash can and waited for a new life to begin. I was impelled by the weight, so I tossed them, keeping only my son's clothes and few personal items and hygiene for myself.

My new life came fast. I was shifted from Vida's house, Robbie's aunt, to Ross Earl's, her uncle, to her Aunt Sharon Ann's spot. It is with Sharon Ann and her friend Marilyn that I lived with my son and was able to enroll in school. I learned Oakland Streets quickly. One thing about living the fast life, the streets hold no fear for a person if they want to make it, and I wanted to make it.

I soon moved out of Sharon Anne's apartment and ended up living with someone else and someone else and someone else, waiting on my welfare case to transfer. I had to get out of the apartment I had rented for myself. The complex I had moved to, I met some people who eventually took me in, trying to help me and my son, not to be on the streets. I don't believe homeless was a technical name then. You were either put out or on the streets. That's what that was called. In the complex, I met several people: Lillian, Pat, Roy, and Wayne (who were brothers); Cal (the manager of the apartments); and Clarence (a brother from the youth center next door). They all were some characters, but it could have been worse. I was eighteen with a bullet and trying to shoot everyone I met but shooting is hard. The thing is tough, and I had never taken target lessons, so I usually was the one who got shot down.

I had no fear of God or these strangers invading my life. I met Jean, Beau, Peewee and Chuck Rowe, Chris Rowe (not related), and so many people that aided in my not-being-put-out-on-the-streets at a price; and eventually, I was not even calling Robbie or Sharon Ann for help. I had a new life with new friends, and that new life quickly turned into a new nightmare. I ended up living with Lillian and her two kids; and things were going pretty well for a minute until one day, when I came home, she had been drinking and attacked me before I was able to get through the door.

I was accused of stealing Lillian's money, twenty dollars, (which her son Woosy later confessed to) but not before we fought. Needless to say, we were put out in the streets, but a neighbor who I had seen in passing let me move in with him until he wanted favors I couldn't give. We were asked to leave his spot as well, and he was nice about it. Thank God he took no for an answer and was not the type to try to make a prostitute out of me. My adventures went on like this for a few months more. Mind you, I only lived in Oakland a year, and this all had happened in the first six months that I lived there. With no money or no prospects, I was at my wits end. All I had to look toward to was the welfare office.

I called the welfare office, and the social worker told me I had four checks waiting on me and that on that very day, she was about to send them back because she hadn't heard from me after my case was transferred and didn't know where to send them. She had mailed them out to the apartment address; and after the mailman seen the other checks still in there when he went to put the other checks in, they all were returned back to them. All the time, I was going through that mess moving here and there, I had never put in a change of address. Another lessoned I learned the hard way always put in a change of address if I had to move. I called Sharon Anne, and she came to get us.

I went on a completely different mission after that. I met Linda, Sharon Ann's cousin who I babysat for; and she allowed me to live at her apartment in the Clinton Park Projects in exchange to take care of her six kids. That worked out until Big Glen came over one day and said we all had to move. Not knowing what I was going to do, in stepped Chris Rowe. By this time, I had been in the projects long enough to meet a few people from sitting outside on the steps, and my life was headed for an even newer twist.

After CPS came to get all the kids, Chris invited me and my son to live with her and her daughter. I started living with Chris; and we became close, good friends and lived off partying (she taught me how to dress fancy), and we lived at the Naval Bases clubbing and going out. It seemed as though my life was turning around for the better. All I was used to was the Flamingo back home, so all that was new to me. I grew up real fast around Chris.

It was through Chris that I met Geraldine. I learned what night life was really about! I mean totally. Men, booze, drugs, sex, money, and you name it; but we weren't prostitutes. But Chris acted like our madam at times. I later found out living there that Geraldine was a committed prostitute, but Chris and I weren't (in our book). My best time in Oakland was around Chris and Gerry. They both believed in God, and I believed they feared Him; but we had so much fun sinning. I had so much fun with them I thought I was in heaven.

John A., Chris's friend, used to keep the kids for us whenever we went out to party. He was crippled on one side and had a curled hand and foot on his left side (it was from birth). All the fun I could have mustered came from living with Chris and hanging with Geraldine. I could not have ever phantom that I would walk into the arms of my Lord and Savior and have my life changed forever being around two of the craziest women I could ever have met, but that is exactly what happened. After all the hell I went through, trying to make a new start in a new city, the best was truly yet to come.

Chris got a flyer one night at a club in Oakland, and on it was featured a group called Tender Love. We ended up going to see the group; and somehow as usual (what Chris wanted she got), Chris met one of the lead singers Rick, and one thing led into a relationship. We all became friends. She made dinner for the group. (She sure could cook, she got me stuck on grits and gravy.) The only time I think she didn't know what she was doing is when she told them *we* could make them outfits to sing in. That was a disaster. By then I told Mark, one of the lead singers that they should find someone else to finish them pants suits.

Eventually, the drama fizzled; and we all moved on. I eventually got my own place on Twenty-Third Street and Foothill, and it is at that place I ran into the manager of Tender Love, Michael. I introduced myself, and we talked and spoke on occasions. Once I guess he felt sorry for me, invited me to see the new King Kong; and he took my son and me to the drive-in. I guess he saw me struggling to go to school and scrape pennies to ride the bus, so he figured I must not have much.

He lived downstairs, and I lived upstairs; and one day, as I was going to school, he was coming in. He stopped me on the stairway and told me of an experience he had in his room. He told me he had seen a cross appear on the wall to him, and he took it as a sign to get his life right, and I should do the same. Well, I thanked him for sharing and went on out the door with my son. After that, I saw him periodically, and he would give me little papers I learned were called *tracts*, to read and he talked about the Seventh-Day Adventist church he was attending. I was like, "Okay, thanks again, bye." But it was eerie to me because I was getting scared, not of him but signs that I'd already had. And for him to be sharing his experience with me was prophetic to me, although I tried to deny that.

Before, I moved to the building on Foothill, my last apartment with Chris and her children was on Ivy drive by Lake Merritt. It was a nice area, not far from the lake in downtown Oakland. We had moved out of the projects and into a nice two-bedroom apartment. *I had a dream of a huge earthquake and the city burning. People were running to and fro as I was standing behind a wall watching when an image of Jesus with outstretched arms appeared in the clouds above the city.* It was as clear as a DVD (and not a bootleg copy either). So I was already having a change in my thoughts and directions, but my living arrangement and present boyfriend at the time dimmed the switch on that vision. So when I ran into Michael and his life-changing experiences, I was greatly affected by his testimony, albeit I pretended not to be; and little did I know just how much of it that would play a major part in my life.

Living with Chris on Ivy Drive was a good time for us. I was in school full time at the College of Alameda. I had met me a soldier, Navy man, Dwight Smith (Suga); and he'd brought along his friend Allan, another Navy guy. Like I said, we frequented a lot of clubs and Naval Bases; and we hooked-up with these two fellas somehow. I met Suga and introduced Allan to Chris, and he and Chris argued all the time and argued up on a baby (Chris Jr. my god-nephew). It was all good like I said until Suga started tripping, and he got crazy and jealous. We fought and made-up and fought until I just had to leave or get Chris kicked out of the apartment.

So that's when I found the Foothill studio apartment, but it was no Ivy Drive. I should have realized God was trying to reach my inner soul, but I wasn't afraid enough I guess, and I put all the *Jesus stuff* behind me still. Suga talked to Chris or somebody I never knew whom; and he found out where I lived, stalked me, and kept coming over unannounced, trying to catch me with someone. I became scared. I called the police on him, and I called my daddy who lived in LA. Once again, I left all my belongings in that apartment, got on the bus, and went to live with my brother Charlie and his wife Odessa.

The day I called the police on Suga (and my son loved him and so did I), he was shocked; but something compelled me to leave. I don't know if it was God or fear or both, but I did not want to be a domestic violence victim. It was what had prompt me to leave Blythe in the first place, getting slapped around by a man. Little did I know this move would be my second movement toward God. The dream being my first, at least to me. My heart wasn't left in San Francisco, but it was oh so close. I left my heart to partying and being promiscuous in Oakland! That year taught me more about life than I could have ever imagined possible.

I just didn't feel the need to party anymore. I was eighteen with a four-year-old son, no welfare, nothing but the clothes on my back end route to new experiences with a new heart and mind and somehow seeking a better state of being, not a better life. I was tired. All the abuse as a child and as an adult, all the partying, being kidnapped, and raped, experimenting with drugs, being *homeless* (in Oakland) had all caught up with me. On the bus, I cried. As I looked down at my baby asleep in my lap, I promised myself. I would never let another man put his hands on me again; and through it all, I didn't know God was cleansing me to accept his truth.

I enrolled in Los Angeles Trade Technical College in 1978. I'd gone to College of Alameda when I was in Oakland, so I had my financial aid transferred and tried to get back on AFDC, Aid to Family with Dependent Children (welfare was called that then).

I left as if I was on a spiritual path. I had dreams and out of body experiences and run into the weirdest people with the strangest messages given to me, either subtly or outright. People would just walk up to me and say, "Do you know you are glowing?" or "Your aura is strong!" and even ask me to *pray for them*. Some would just stare. Once on the bus, a man was talking to me and said, "Ooh, an evil face just crossed your face." We'd been talking about God and goodness. As I look back now, I believe it was that old me trying to shut him up and scare him. The devil in me might have known God was winning my soul back.

I began getting invitations to various church functions. I searched Sunday church services directories to attend. I had a spirit of fear within me that would not allow me to sleep. I kept thinking something was going to happen to me. I felt death. I lived this way for a long time once I left Oakland. I moved to the Stephen Hotel in downtown Los Angeles on Flower Street and met Darlene Gist who taught me tap moves and how to survive (Richard Crenna from the Real McCoy's, would visit his mom there, may they both rest in peace), and I would sleep in the lobby because I was afraid to read my Bible alone and be alone. But I had an urgency to read it. I know now the enemy knew I was leaving his side of the street. I was crossing over.

When I left downtown LA, I went to live at my brother's again on Forty-Fifth Street and Hooper. It was here that I became reacquainted with two of my childhood friends, Raymond Whitten and Alvin Jacocks. I hadn't seen them in years. Raymond use to always mess with me with his little nasty self, but it was Alvin that I wish I could have talked too. I had just gotten out of a bad relationship and was not thinking of romance at that time. Alvin was like my ship lost at sea. I never could connect to him, and I to this day wonder why. He is a mystery to me.

I took the bus everywhere, met all kinds of people. One day, while standing on the bus stop, a big white Brougham Cadillac pulled up beside me. I thought it was a pimp trying to push up on me. My first thought was I thought I left all this kind of mess in Oak Town. To my disbelief, it was some of my old Navy friends, Bear, from Oakland! What were the odds of that? We kicked it at the bus stop for a few minutes and exchanged information, and I never saw him again.

One day, on my way to Los Angeles City College, I took the bus on Vermont that would take me to Melrose. It was a crowd of people at the bus stop, and I was talking to one lady casually when the bus came we got on. She went her way to find a seat, and I sat in the front on the west side of the bus, facing north. As the doors were closing, a lady squeezed through them to stop them from closing. When she got on the bus, she sat next to me and smiled; and she started making small talk with me. I was trying to be nice, but I didn't want to talk.

I first thought she looked like someone I knew from Blythe. Then she reminded me of my Aunt Mandy's sister, Aunt Rebecca in Texas. Then she looked like Ms. Ruby in Blythe (not Cavers). She had a long nose with a mole on her face—sort of *witchified* but not *ugly-fied*—and as my mind was going in this negative direction (I was about to miss my blessing), she started talking about church. Excited, I told her about my dreams and visions, and she gave me a tract to read with the address of the church she attended on it. I was loosening up to her when she arose to leave she said, "I'm Sister Lottie Devine, and if you can come this Saturday to church, we'll be glad to have you," and she turned to exit as the bus stopped. The doors open, and she was gone. I looked at her mingle into the crowd of people and realized she'd only ridden a block, but it seemed we'd talked all my life. I had no clue. God had just used her to change my life.

That Saturday, I went to her church; and they were having a five-day no-smoking van there. I'd seen that van in a dream but didn't know what it was in my dream. I walked into that little church and saw the doves on the red cloth across the podium in the same position as in it was in my dream, and I got chills. I went to sit down along with my son, and I felt a tap on my shoulder midway into the service. It was Sharon Anne from Oakland, sitting with her cousin who I was introduced to later as sister Elizabeth McKinzey (RIP); and I was amazed! I still didn't see God in all this.

As the song service began, I was waiting for that Hurricane to arise in the pit of my stomach; but it never came. I didn't even clap.

It was a good song service. No one turning flips and doing hurdles or running up and down the aisles, so I was just content sitting there. But it was a family sitting behind me, and this lady was singing loud, and I could tell she was enjoying herself as though she was so glad to be in church. I didn't have the heart to tell her to *get up outta my ears.* (I learned later it was her first time there too, and her name was Barbara Jackson, and we became best of friends.)

When the Pastor, Orlando Rudley Jr., got up to welcome the first-time visitors and later preached, my stomach went crazy. I felt like jumping out my seat. As I sat through his sermon, my heart started pounding more and more until finally, when he asked if any-one wants to give their life to God to come forward, I thought I was being pulled out of my seat. I didn't want to go to the altar! But I couldn't just sit there, seems like the longer I sat, the more the blood pounded in my veins. *This had to be the Spirit,* I told myself, urging me to get up. My son and I, Barbara and her family, her son Bea and husband Bear (not my friend Bear), walked there as well! It was more people, but all I knew was I was there. I had finally found my home church.

I didn't know what to expect when I got off the Avalon bus and rode it to Forty-Second Street that Saturday, Sabbath. I learned it was called and walked that sidewalk to Greater Mid-City Seventh-Day Adventist Church, but when I turned that corner and saw that van, I had an overwhelming feeling. I was in the right place and I knew that God had directed my path to his Truth through my dreams and visions. I walked many sidewalks day and night to get there that day, not to Him because He was with me all the time, but I just didn't know it. The dreams and visions were His way of bringing me out of the streets and into His fold in a way that when His call came for me to repent, I would know it was His call. I still have a lot of street in me; but I'm not ashamed of it because if it had not been for me being in the streets, I never would have met Sister Devine or Michael for that matter. I read those cute little Bible stories books as a child, my mother used to get from people stopping by the house to leave the big blue books with colorful pages (not the Jehovah Witnesses ones, although they have similar ones), and they were made by Adventist companies. When I saw the books on the shelves at the church, I marveled then I knew my search for the truth brought me to the Adventist denomination, and I was where I needed to be.

I call myself a street Ventist because as I studied more and more with Sister Devine and later learned about the Sabbath and the health message and what generational Adventism was, I realized that although I may have had to find the truth by hook or crook, by alley ways and beatings, by drugs and abusive relationships, by avenues and dark streets, I am no lesser a child of God than anyone who was *born* into an Adventist family. What is more import than that is that I *was lost but now I am found. God led me to him. That means He wanted me just as much as He wanted anyone who think you have to be born into an Adventist family to love the Lord.* And I believe, "And ye shall now the truth, and the truth shall make you free!" (John 8:32). And these are scriptures I claim in truth. Amen.

My family may or may not have feared God or may not have come to hear Him as I have, but I know when I read II Timothy 1:2–7, it is what my grandmother and mother gave me, to learn to love the Lord, and they made sure that I did love him by reading the scriptures. Whether my parents feared God or not, it was not my business, they made us go to church. I should be only concern that they took the time out of their street lives to put us on a path that would give me the best education of all, and that is to love God and know Jesus and trust His Holy Spirit. That fear is a fear of respect. That's what we are called to do to preach the Gospel, and a person does not have to become a Seventh-Day Adventist to do so nor be a generational Adventist at that. I am what God has called me to be. One who goes into the streets to tell the world of his advent. His soon coming. I am a Street-Ventist and my grandmother and mother helped to make that possible, teaching me the golden rule of life.

PS.
Thanks, Mama
Thanks, Big Mama (RIP)

Genie

"I now pronounce you man and wife."

Wow, I thought as the preacher said those final words. I was actually married to Genie, *Po' Red,* as he was known in the *hood*. I didn't even know his real name until we were reunited in 1997, and we were married February 12, 1999. Genie was a real thug. He used to scare me when we were kids, but he was fun to be around. He wasn't like the other boys around the park. He was always with the big boys or by himself. He was always looking at people sideways and would cuss you out in a minute. He didn't take no stuff off people. He didn't care who it was. When he did decided to play with us, the local kids and myself, he always had some cool stories to tell about what he had done or where he had been. He was nasty too. Genie was the kind of nasty that made us girls giggle and run from him and hoping to get caught by him, always trying to touch somebody's butt or pull up a skirt. He was always targeting me especially, but I could run. I was quick. Genie had a way of popping out his knee. I didn't know he was double jointed then; and I would scream, then he would walk off, dipping in his little *gangstah-pinp* walk as though he was cool, and I just thought he was.

To be honest, I don't know how in the world this day happened; but Brenda Williams and I was in the park. We always hung together especially when there was no school. Genie just happened to be in the park on that day as well. He came over to where we were playing; and being his usually self, he started messing with us. We double teamed him and took off running and that day, turned into one long summer's run. From that day forward, every time he saw us, he would chase us then other boys joined in; and other girls played along. Before we knew it, there were a number of boys and girls running through the city of Los Angeles all over the place. We ran through Trinity Park down Twenty-Fifth Street on San Pedro Street on Central even as far as to Twenty-Eighth Street school and back around by Washington near San Pedro Street School. People in and out of the stores around us were looking at us as though we were rioters until they saw us laughing and fighting off the boys. It was incredulous! It was the best summer I ever had in my childhood in LA. The boys were trying to get us in bushes and behind houses and in cubby holes, all to get quick grinds on us girls. We screamed and hid from them and fought them off and fell getting away from them and just giggle our silly little selves into a frenzy. We only allow those to catch us who we liked.

I grew up with some pretty decent-looking young men. I had a crush on about fifty percent of them, but I was a tomboy. I liked climbing trees and fighting. I would go to the park and play tether ball with the girls from time to time, but I loved playing on the Carrom Game Board and throwing the football and getting up baseball games. I loved living near Trinity Park. It was always something to do; and when we weren't at Trinity Park, we would go to All Peoples and hang out. I liked hanging with Brenda because she was like me, down and ready for anything. She came from a family with a lot of brothers, and I only had two boys in my family, but I tried to do everything they did. Genie intrigued me 'cause he was bad. There were other bad boys who came around; but with Genie, you can see badness walking beside him as though they were twins.

I think of that time because it was the one time that mostly all the kids in the neighborhood actually spent that much time together. I know Brenda Whitten and I used to follow her brother Raymond and Wayne Foster all over town too when he would let us. He and I called ourselves liking each other once as well. We would walk to downtown Los Angeles, stopping in places, stealing clothes and candy whatever we could. We were going to the Metropolitan Swimming pool one day and ran up some stairs of this building on Washington and Maple and grabbed a hand full of bathing suits they were making inside, and they were all tops! I think Brenda might have grab a few actual sets. We ran like the wind blows on a windy day, cutting in between traffic. People blowing their horns at us. We didn't care. We were having fun. There was another time, we all decided to walk to Exposition Park. I don't know if Barry Stone was with us that day or not; but I know Raymond, his sister Brenda, and I went; and we explored every building on that route, hopped any fence we felt we had to and stole out of any store that would let us in it. When we finally made it to the Sports Arena, it just so happened the Ringling Bros. Circus was preparing for a show; and in the back of the Arena, they were unloading the animals. We ran to stand on the rails to watch. We saw them unload bears and monkeys and a lion. When the lion was being unloaded, we started making growling noises and just being obnoxious. Brenda got scared and was ready to go. The men handling the animals were trying to make us leave and hush, but we kept on until a guard was called to get rid of us, and we all took off running and laughing.

We had some good times in our hoods. From the streets by Forty-First and Maple to Eighteenth Street and Washington on back to Adams and Maple. Our lives were meshed either by school or family. The guys who I was raised around were some of the best fellows ever. I wouldn't change anything about my growing up with them; and the girls, I had some pretty cool friends and still do. Many of us never saw each other again after those times especially that big run in the city we had. It was like seeing the running of the bulls in retrospect. We were so young and innocent (to a degree), then times changed and drugs and gangs took life to another level; and things had changed all over the world. Some of them died too young, got on drugs, got married and had kids, went off to school, some went to the army, some to jail and prison, some found good jobs, and some just stayed in the hood to grow old. I left because I needed to at the time. One of my deepest regrets was not staying around to get better acquainted with one of my playmates, Alvin Jacocks. He was a school-girl crush that I wish could have been more than what it was; but circumstance in my life led me far away from him. He became like a ship lost at sea to me. I don't know if it was wrecked, or it's still floating along the ocean somewhere, or that it washed ashore on a distant island, waiting to be found again.

I found myself knocking on Genie's mother's door. My friend Gwen, who I hadn't seen in many years and ran across, told me where he lived. Gwen and Bennie lived around the corner from him, and I went by there. I hadn't seen Bennie Leggett since Gwen and I lived on Fifty-Ninth and Bonsallo when he had brought one of homeboys Peewee over to see me.

Gwen had told me, "Girl, gone around there and surprise his ass. If you see that little brown car in the driveway, his ass there." And gave that little crazy laugh that she have, and we hugged, and I left. So with the feeling as though a thousand lady bugs was crawling over my arms and inside my stomach, I rode around there and knocked.

Soon as I was getting ready to say hello is anybody there, I heard his mother voice say, "Gene! Come get the door. Somebody just walked up." Then he appeared and said my whole name in a slow drawl, "Ar-lene Rog-ers."

I made small talk with him, "Why you got to say all my name?" And he laughed as he was coming out the door combing his afro. He hugged me, and his mother asked him who was it, and he introduced us. I peeked in the door and said hello and went to shake her hand; and he followed me saying, "This my wife."

I laughed, and his mother looked me up and down, smiling, and she said, "Well, I say."

Then after I told her it was nice meeting her, I walked back outside. With Genie in tow, I said "Hey, Genie, do you remember when we were running all over the streets, me, you and Brenda, and the others?"

And he smile and looked at me sideways and said, "Yes, I do, think about it a lot. Do I have to chase you now?"

I smiled and said, "I don't know. Do you?" I got in my car, and as he closed the door for me and requested my number, I scribbled it down on some paper to hand to him. He bent in the car and kissed me on the cheek and said, "I meant what I said. You gone be my wife."

I smiled and backed out of the driveway and watched him watching me.

In the Den of Lost Angels

Dedicated to Peewee

In the Bible, Jesus said, "I was naked, and ye clothed me. I was sick, and ye visited me. I was in prison, and ye came unto me" (Matthew 25:36 KJV).

Throughout history concerning religion, *imprisonment and abuse* has gone hand in hand. Many of Christs' followers and true disciples were incarcerated or abused. Stephen, who has been labeled as *the first martyred* disciple of Christs', was stoned to death for not denouncing his belief in Christ Jesus; and his death according to a recent website I visited, bible.org, recited that Stephen's death meant so much to the Christian movement that his and Christs' deaths are the only ones mentioned in the bible. Peter who was one of Christs' boldest followers was jailed, as was Paul the Roman soldier who converted to Christianity after *slaying and abusing* countless Christians under the Roman Government rule. No one, especially Jesus, ever said that to be a Christian, picking up His cross would be easy. Plus, He said to carry our own cross and live by *His example.*

I never went to jail for being a believer in Christ. I went to jail because I disobeyed Christs' teachings. I lived my life my way and not by his commandments. I gave the judicial system fifteen years of my life over a period of times; and the enemy of Jesus Christ, the majority of what was spent in the *free world.* Drugs, promiscuity, fast living, and petty hustling was more of a draw for me than serving God in a *church house.* I accepted Christ in my heart and as my personal Savior as it were at a very young age but the allurement of growing up and the changes in my body and mind and hanging out with my *friends* and experimenting with life in the fast lane, appeared to be more promising to me. Especially that we were in the 1960s growing up, when love, peace and drugs, were ripening in societies around California and across the world. The Hippie movement, the Black Panthers, and Black exploitation movies were on the rise; and we kids were taken it all in. And with that rise, it seemed as though I had begun a race with the devil that had almost certainly kept me away from the Lord rather than lead me to Him.

I was young and mischievous, curious and uninhibited. I fought kids at school and in parks and experimented with drugs and alcohol that was plentiful in my neighborhood. I was suspended from school regularly and was fast becoming known as a *problem child*. I had no clue about abuse and statistics. I had no social workers to intervene in my life to try to help me to understand what I was feeling or what I was thinking. Child Protective Services was not a driving force in the lives of children as it has become in cities and states around the world. What I went through growing up and those who suffered the same existences, we had to *rough it*. I can count the kids on my finger who I was able to talk to about what was happening in my life, and they were going through the same things, over caring *uncles, fathers, and friends of the family*. I was a walking statistic, victim and survivor. My life had gone from top student to top criminal; and by the time I had turned twenty-one, I was headed toward a life of degradation and criminal roads I would travel that I never would have imagined I would travel down. Jesus was in the kitchen stove of my heart, on the back burner without any fire under the pot.

By the time that I was in my thirties, I had become a survivor of abuse, of cancer, of drug addiction, bad relationships, and a survivor of the penal system. In 1997, I was paroled off a state number from California Rehabilitation Center (CRC) in Norco, California. It would be my second parole. The first being in 1992 from the California Institution for Women (CIW). I had graduated from the county jails. I paroled from Blythe California as well. I had went to Blythe to start a new life, even had another child, a little boy, and ended up starting a new life of crime and dissension, camouflaged in recovery.

In 1996, I enrolled in a recovery program, The Gibson House for Women, in San Bernardino, California and completed the program in fifty-four days and went to a sober living called A Better Choice in Rubidoux California operated by Brenda Jones and eventually left there to work with a Pastor name Michael Ashley. It was that road leading to the unknown, or the road that lead back to the prison. My parole officer had made that clear. It was while I was involved with GH and Pastor Ashley that my future took a turn for what seemed like a positive outlook and a promised total life change. Between receiving a recovery program and working in the church with Pastor Ashley, the fog had lifted as they say in recovery; and I could see a light house ahead, and my feet were pointed in the direction of that light.

While I was in Gibson House, I had gotten in touch with Pastor Martin Howard who had been coming to Blythe to pastor my mom's church. It was while attending the church one day in Blythe at one of the members request, Sister Betty Howard (no relation to the pastor), that I met Pastor Ashley. He had come to speak; and during his appeal, I felt overwhelmed and cried through the whole moment. Sister Audrey Howard (the pastor's wife) hugged me and told to me to speak with her husband after the service and see what he could do for me. Had I been in my right mind, I would have known that sister Betty asking me to come hear pastor Ashley speak that day was the tip of the iceberg of the Lord intervening in my life. For at one point in the service, Ashley sang a song; and when he sang, I recognized his voice and looked at him closely and saw that the Pastor Ashley was the Michael I had met in Oakland, California when I had first left Blythe in my senior year of high school.

While living in Oakland, I ad frequented many clubs and parties; and at one of those clubs, I had met a young lady name Chris. She loved to party; and one night, we went out. We met some guys in a group called Tender Love. Michael was the manager and opening act. I never known his last name; so when Sister Betty asked me to come hear, Pastor Ashley from her San Bernardino church speak. It never dawned on me. It would be Michael from Tender Love.

One day, after a group at Gibson House, one of the girls called me to the bulletin wall and showed me a paper that had *Clients Rights* in bold capital letters for those who were clients in the recovery home. While there clean, I had often lead the girls out in worship or sang songs for them. When we had *free time* and according to the clients rights notice, I had the right to leave the home to go to church. A right they didn't advertise. I later found out because some of the girls had used that as an excuse and not come back. I was not trying to *escape*. I was there by *order* of my parole officer and grateful, I could have been incarcerated again, so I made the necessary arrangements and went to church.

After the service, the day I was reunited with Ashley, and Pastor Howard; and Pastor Ashley had both agree that once I made it to San Bernardino, contact them, and they would help me. When I found out about the right to go to church, I contacted them, told them where I was at, and a van pool was sent to get me one Saturday (Sabbath). I went to Sixteenth Street Seventh-Day Adventist Church and stayed all day. It was my first and last visit. I had become so caught up in the service and the moment and the taking other passengers to their respective homes that when I returned to Gibson House, it was dark after 5:00 p.m., and the place was in a panic. The staff thought I had run.

A meeting (it was called a special) was called with the staff and the clients, and they had to decide my truth. If I could stay, had I gotten high; and basically, they needed to know what *was I thinking*. I explained to them that the service had been over at two. They had dinner. The van had other members to take to their houses, and then I was brought to Gibson House. I explained to them that that was how *we had church*! Needless to say, in order to stay in the program, I had to revoke going to any future services while in the home there; and I had *special* duties. I had to journal my actions and bring it to primary (our morning group). I was willing to do anything to not go back to prison, so I accepted the terms; but I still believe that the house manager didn't want to do the paper work every week that it took to allow me to go on those passes. She subliminally turned the *special meeting* into the direction of me not going to church at all.

I left GH honorably; and after attending a transitional home, the ABC homes, I began working with Pastor Ashley with his Prison Ministry Organization. He had acquired some land in Rialto California and open two half way- houses on the same property as New Beginnings for men and women respectively and I became the supervisor of both. I worked for room and board in the beginning and then was awarded a $400 stipend to help me with necessities. The clientele were men and women who were coming from prison or jail, who had instructions from their parole officer or court orders to be in a facility. Between both houses twenty-five people were housed. It was an awesome experience, and I had one and a half years clean when I began working there and four years clean and sober when the facility closed in 2001. I later went on to having eight years clean and sober getting married and going to two schools and buying a car and going to church on a steady basis; and then in 2004, I relapsed during a time when it seemed as though I was living *my life like it was golden.*

I say that my life was camouflage in recovery because I had everything. A new child, a good job, going to school, a car, a home (had gotten married), and everything just seemed so right. While I was living at New Beginnings, I learned so much about the bible. Through bible studies with Pastor Ashley, supervising and running groups for the men and women, I felt I was ready for the real world. I was attending classes at San Bernardino Valley College for Human Services and Alcohol and Drug Counseling, so this arrangement with the pastor was like being on the job with training for real. I was welcomed back into the prison I had once walked the sidewalks of. While at CRC, I met Cynthia Fonseca in vocational offset printing, and Bob Frazier, Marlene Pou, and Pam Brown through the Arts-N-Correction prison program. It was through them my opportunities to survive seem to have opened. For it was through their leaderships, I became in touch with my artistic side and abilities to lead. They put me in charge of various programs and brought me *into the presence of the woman hiding inside of me* through art and printing. (I was in charge of the designs and layouts.)

I call the prisons Dens of Angels because I went back as a counselor and volunteered, I found that so many of the women truly believed in God, and they weren't pretending. They were sincerely seeking a change in their lives. It was a glorious feeling to experience re-entry into the prison on the *other* side, successful and focused. After completion of my main courses for my Associate in Arts Degree in Human Services, I was able to get *in-house* hands on work through a company named Civigencs. I would become a pre-certified counselor as a trainee at the California Institute for men's (CIM) prison in Chino, California. I thought I was a biscuit rising. I was nice, brown, and crisped. I was ready. I later left Civigenics for a higher paid position at my old joint CRC and worked for Walden House, another prison-based recovery program. I worked as a counselor. We were called SAP counselors (substance abuse program counselors). For two months and then became a supervisor until my mother became gravely ill, and I had to quit. The rollercoaster I was riding had begun to speed up; and I was holding on but only by the seat of my pants, my hands were free and seemed to have decided, that to pick up a pipe (to smoke cocaine) again would show me the way how to stop the ride.

This decision caused the biscuits in the oven that were rising to deflate and burn. All my aspirations, hopes, and cars; my house, and my family took a turn for the worse. The struggle to get to eight years in sobriety was a hard road, but I had made it, but I was rising up to fast. The fire in my oven was too high, and I was doing great things for myself and the community, but I didn't have enough of the Lord in me to run to Him when I needed too. Hence, I say I was like a biscuit in the oven too long that burned. I had burnt myself out; and when I needed the strength to go on, I couldn't find it, not in myself, not in recovery, not even in God.

Working in the Den of Lost Angels and living in the den of lost angels was one of the greatest experiences of my life. I know it sounds strange for me to say being in prison and working in prison was good; but for me, it and the people that God put in my path shaped my life. I was walking around with the Manson girls (Helter Skelter/Charles Manson), women who killed their babies, their husbands, lovers, you name it, women killers. The guards were sneaking in items to give the girls, having sex with them, and beating them, girls loving other girls. It was a world within the world, and I had become a part of it. It opened my eyes to a reality I would never have known existed had I not gone in there myself. I am sure there could have been other ways to meet reality; but for the road I had chosen, my reality came in the form of incarceration. As it is said in the recovery programs, "…jails, institutions, and death." I realized through these affiliations the death had to be next unless I changed; and inside of me, I knew I needed a miracle to change.

It was such a powerful atmosphere behind the wall, the Den of Lost Angels; and it is because God, through His infinite grace and mercy and abounding love, shows up daily to those men and women. He showed up while I was there as well. His love and His grace reached into the depths of my soul, of my disparity; and He began to break down the strongholds that bound me. That is why when I got out, I had said I would never forget the brothers and sisters I met along the way; and then God lead me to the Afican AME church in Blythe, to a future I had no clue would introduce me to a ministry that I could fulfill that promise, Touch of Love Prison Ministry.

The Lord says, "Take heed that ye despise not one of these little ones. For I say to you that in Heaven their angels do always behold the face of my Father which is in heaven. For the Son of Man come to save that which was lost." (Matthew 18:10 and 11). While I twisted and turned along my road to recovery, I found solice in the scriptures. It wasn't until I found myself lost and alone all over again that I realized reading the scriptures were key, but having a *true personal relationship* with Jesus was the golden key to a more productive life on the road to salvation. I did community service. I got cleaned from drugs. I took a different view on dating, and my social environment changed. I visited the sick and took the message of hope to the men and women prisons; but with all that I was doing, Jesus and I was not in a relationship. We were acquaintances, and that nearly cost me my life.

My miracle came after I relapsed. I know it is said in recovery that not everyone has a relapse, and I have seen that happen. I have seen people walk out of programs only to be found dead in the streets, in hotels, wrecks, and so on chasing that one last high. That was my miracle. My relapse did not lead me to death. It led me to *change*. It lead me to a direct path to Jesus. I have been through the fire, and I go boldly to the throne of God today. I can't do or undo what I've done in the past, but I am grateful I have Jesus in my life today and see only Him in my future. I was lost, but now I'm found. (Luke 15:7, "And I give God all the glory for how my life has come full circle.") I used to be afraid to say that my life had come full circle because I thought I was going to die, as a completed life cycle; but one day, I was with my grandkids, and I had bought some *bubbles* to blow with them. As I was blowing, a large bubble had come from the little plastic gadget that looks like a magnifying glass; and as I was blowing, another bubble came out of the big one and went into the atmosphere. And I thought, that's my life. I am not about to die from the life I had known. I was evolving from it, and I was about to go into a new direction. I had a feeling that I was about to *rise above* in my new life.

I truly believe that my brothers and sisters incarcerated have a power that is as strong and as binding in the Lord as we who are in *the free world.* The Lord says so in Matthew 18:20, "Where two or three are gathered together in my name, I am there in the midst of them." And it is with this belief I know there is always hope for God's children wherever they reside. Therefore, if we are imprisoned in our minds by jail or by drugs, sex or desires, know that there is a way out in Christ. (See 1 John 2:1.) The Scripture reads that, "I can do all things through Christ who strengthens me" (Philippians 4:13). I learned this the hard way, but I am grateful that I was able to learn that; and I know one day, every sidewalk that I have walked on, every road that I have traveled upon, will not be anything to me if it has not led me to the golden sidewalks of the kingdom of God.

Crack Mama

(To my queens who have lost their reign and regained it,
and to those who have died along the way)

C rack cocaine, hit the hoods hard; and I remember I said I would *never* stoop to that level and be found smoking *that mess*. Well I stooped and waddled and rolled all in it. I was a sherm smoker, and I drank and on *occasions*. I tooted coke. Sherm was a form of angel dust. Many called it animal tranquilizer, and tooting coke was short for sniffing it up ones nose. By the time *free-basing* came to the hoods of America, the rap game was in full swing. The gang-bangers were *ballin'* as it was deemed, and the jails were being filled with a new breed of criminals, and it all didn't miss me.

The one thing I didn't like about being out in the *game* was the challenges there were of being a better drug dealer, a better hoe, a better thief, or a better whatever. It was always somebody out to get someone. It was scary, but it was fun. Or so I believed it was, I had no perception of where living in the fast lane would take me. I went to places I never thought I would go, was with people I never thought I would be with, and lived in places that I would never have lived in if I could have helped it. I sold myself. I sold drugs. I stole from stores and even attempted a few robberies. I should have known then that God was with me because every Robbery I attempted was foiled. Every major crime I tried to be a part of, something went wrong. *God was trying to tell me something* indeed, but I wasn't hearing it. Many of the people I had hung with, died or was imprisoned, or the drugs never let them go. I say drugs, but I realize now it was the demons within. Some of us keep our demons very close to us until they take over our whole being. Whatever God has planned for me, it did not require that I be consumed by my demons.

I walked the sidewalks at night to get drugs, booze, get laid, get beat up, or to go beat up someone else. I had to beg on the streets when I had messed up my money and had no food to eat or place to lay my head. I could have gone home, but I didn't want to miss getting *high.* I let men misuse my mind and body and allowed emotional stress to keep me in the bondage of a drug-addicted life; but what I recall is that through it all, a voice inside of me kept telling me that *I didn't have to live like this.* When I would get high, I would talk about God and living right and people would be turned off by it. Some would call me a hypocrite, and some would listen. I didn't try to be a *spiritual guru in the jungle,* but the presence of God was that powerful inside of me, and I still ignored it.

I have nearly lost my life behind these elements trying to escape reality and ride the fence of indecisiveness, trying to serve *two masters* (Matthew 6:24), actually three: God, the devil, and my own views of how I thought I should live. I saw many women including myself lose their hope and became misguided, and some even succumbed with those faded hopes and dreams they may have had at one time in their lives. I think the difference between them and me is *I never lost my hope.*

I can't count the times that I passed death on the sidewalks of Blythe, California; Oakland, California; and Los Angeles; San Bernardino; Pomona, and other cities I visited. I was not always looking for crack; but drugs, none the same, men, parties, and other things that I thought would sustain me. I was living day by day as though I had no kids, no family, and no destination with no point of return. If I had died, I wasn't worried about heaven or hell. God or the devil, all I cared about my next fix, hit or drink, even sex became a burden. All I wanted was to stay in the stupor of being out of my mind. I didn't want to think. Jesus only came of my mouth if I was running for my life or having good sex. And more times than good sex, I was running for my life.

I didn't know about all things working together for the good. (See Romans 8:28.) All I knew was that there was not anything good working for me in those streets. I didn't believe that God was even in my life anymore. I didn't see near-death experiences as having divine interventions. I saw them as being slick enough to escape or sly enough to *get over*. I didn't know Jesus. All the church experiences of my life did not prepare me for the life I would have roaming the streets. I came to believe the old saying, *God takes care of babies and fools*, that's as bout as much recollection of the bible I had in me; and that was not even a scripture.

I was in and out of the judicial system for a better part of fifteen years, and it was not until 1993 that I began hearing terms like *crack head, crack mama, strawberry and chicken-heads, to the curb, and tweaking*. These were all very derogatory words and phrases to me, but I had placed myself in the categories to be referred as such or caught displaying actions that deemed me a *tweaker* or supposedly *shot to the curb*. They all alluded to a woman in particular who sold her body for *anything,* from a hit off the crack pipe to a bite of food, to a place to stay. It had become that serious for some. I didn't consider myself as any one of that because I knew where I had come from, and my mama hadn't raised me like that. I demanded respect, and I tried to give it. I may have done some of those things, but some of them I had been doing way before I became addicted. I say that in defense of my childhood games when boys would say, "If you give me a kiss you can lick my lollipop." Tongue in cheek I write that because I see that as a pre training to sinful living, and my respect to so called *crack mamas* runs deeply. There were those of us out there that had to do what we had to do to survive. Some just laid down and rolled with the punches. I praise God every day for Him giving me insight and boldness and credibility out there in them streets. I was able to keep what little dignity I had before I was a so–called crack head. I would fight if someone called me a crack head or anything besides my name. I just never saw myself as that I was just someone who had made the wrong choices in life, and those choices had brought me from the child my mama had birth and had high hopes for, to a woman who needed help and a spiritual miracle, mind, body, and soul. Being called those names only weaken the mind of those beautiful sisters more, and there were more crack daddies as there were women. Men had turned just as *hoe-ish* and to the curb as women. That crack cocaine did not discriminate.

I met some pretty incredible woman while I was out in the streets in diverse places. Mothers struggling to care for themselves and their children. Women who never graduated from high school but had IQ's above mine, and I had three degrees. Some had jobs and worked the streets at night either by prostitution or hustling in the dope-game. Many would give you the shirt off their backs and knew more about God than myself or many of the preachers I had heard in my young life. Many of the women told me repeatedly that I didn't belong out there and for that, they treated me with great respect and watched over me as one of their own. I had become one of them, for as I might have looked like *Sister Mary Patrick. I was Deloris Van Carthier underneath my skin* (sister act).

Being called a crack mama bothered me, but I didn't let it tear me down because I knew I had placed myself in that predicament to be called such. I had fallen in the cracks of life, with no hope, no aspirations, and nothing to challenge me but family's disappointment in me; and that wasn't enough to change me. Then God opened my eyes and saw fit to take the scales off my eyes and the wax out my ears to see and hear His voice. He made it so that when I heard the voice speaking to me, I would know it was *Him.* My life was turned around just as fast as I had put myself in addiction's tornado; and it took me around and around until God said I had had enough. And He told the storms in my life, *Peace be still*; and I was freed. *And I am free.*

I don't know how my life would have been if I wasn't molested or unsupported in my endeavors to be *somebody*; but I don't blame anyone, not even myself. I made choices in an adult world with a child's mentality; and while death passed me by, God had me in His arms all the time, down every sidewalk my feet pitted and patted. I had Him beside me every step. When God finally sat me down to talk with Him, I realized I was never alone out there in those streets. I was standing in Jesus' shadow being shielded and protected by His blood. Once I made up my mind to follow Him, to make Him my personal savior, I thanked him for every trial that I had gone through and road that I had taken because I reasoned, if walking those sidewalks lead me to Him, then all I can say is Hallelujah! I learned to stop following the fun.

Refining Me

I painted a picture during my struggles to abstain from drugs and trying to find some normalcy to my life. It was a colorful self-portrait depicting my relapses and my rediscovery of recovery. It was my acknowledgement of needing Jesus in my life and my hope to get a grip on my life. It was an inanimate piece, although after painting it my miracle did not happen in a profound way. There was no earth shaking moments, but I knew I was walking through a tunnel that shone a light at the other end, and I felt if I could make it to that point. I would find victory waiting for me.

I am living in that victory at the time of this writing (2009), but that all happen in 2007. My mother's death in 2008 took me by surprise. It jolted me and rocked me and rattled my cage and stepped on my toes, and it was a sigh of relief all at the same time because I knew she was free. She had no more pain, no more feeling incompetent, and no more having to worry about me. I felt as though I had been robbed of her. I knew she would pass soon but not without me by her side; so on top of everything else, I had a guilty feeling within me that I had let her down. Not a guiltiness of how my life had been lived but of the promise I had made her that I would never put her in a home. I wanted to be by her side whenever she was ready to walk through her last tunnel; and before I knew it, she was gone alone and in a strange place.

All I have are my memories of my mother. My youngest son, Bertheno, once remarked, "She has no headstone. Her stuff was burned up in a fire. She's just gone. *It's like she never existed.*"

And at that particular time, all I could say in a melancholy tone was, "Huh," in acknowledgement that he was poetically yet hauntingly right; but given that response that I did, I look back and see that we both needed answers. And that was his way of saying that he did. We both know that she existed and would continue to do so in our memories and in our kids and in all that we have been taught because she was in each and every one of us somehow.

I remember as a toddler in Blythe, California, I sat on the steps of my Uncle Arthur's trailer, sipping hot coffee. Well, I had intentions of sipping it anyway. My Aunt Lucille (Uncle Arthur's wife) had given me a cup of coffee and told me that it was hot. "Let it cool." I remember her saying it clearly; and then she sat it beside me and walked into the door of the trailer. Honestly, when I recall these childhood memories, I can't help but feel that God knew I was going to write about them at a later point in time. My mother used to be amazed at the things I could recall that she had forgotten all about, especially flashbacks when I was two and three years old.

The coffee was a beautiful color brown. That coffee gets when milk is added to it, and the smoke was dancing hypnotically from the cup and into the atmosphere, luring me, and I kept *watching* for it to cool off. I guess I saw the smoke disappear one to many times and felt it was cool enough to drink and picked up the cup, but the cup was still hot; and as I tried to place it down quickly, it spilled and ran all over the step where I sat and I wailed. It must have been a good one because my uncle Arthur had come to me very quickly, and all I can remember is him picking me up out of that hot coffee and rushing me around to my grandmothers' house. My grandmother was our Big Mama. Everyone called her that, but her name was Irene, and the grown-ups called her *Rene*. As he was running me around there, he was calling her by her name, "Rene!" Aunt Lucille had trailed behind him; as I grew older, and they told their versions, my mother said Aunt Lucille was saying over and over how sorry she was; and my uncle Arthur, whose pet I was, cussed her out and told her she should never have given me the coffee.

I was three or four when that happened, and I remember my mother reaching for me. They were trying to undress me to get the

SIDEWALK TALES

wet clothes off of me. I was in my underwear and a T-shirt to begin
with. We didn't have sidewalks in Jackson Courts where we lived. It
was a piece of property that Mr. and Mrs. Jackson had their house
on, and a few other big ones and some shanties they had for the men
in the harvest to live in with a community shower structure as well.
The front entrance from Uncle Arthur's trailer was a dirt and gravel
road that lead to the back houses and little apartments. Gravel was in
all the yards, with some patches of grass here and there and big trees
that cast shade that the men and women sat under on hot and cool
days, drinking and talking and listening to music. It was later told to
me that my mother hit that gravel so fast once she saw me blistering
up, and she got me to the hospital. I don't know how she got me
there, but I do remember coming home with a bandaged *booty*, and
I could not sit down for a long time!

When I had realized the cup was too hot and was trying to sit it
back down, the pain seared through my hands; and I shook the cup.
The coffee spilled on my hands, and I dropped the cup which cause
the coffee to splatter on my thighs and in between my legs. When I
went to stand up, I sat back down into the spill on the steps. I prob-
ably was in shock. To this day, I have that coffee stain imprinted on
my behind and my thighs and portions of my legs and near my pri-
vate area. My mother later told me that I was treated for first degree
burns and a few blistered spots; and that the doctor said I was very
lucky because my skin was so tender. It could have been worse. As
I look back on that day and knowing how my body looks today, no
ugly burn scars, I know that I was blessed. God was shielding me
even then. Today I sport a permanent tattoo of a map on my butt and
toward my leg. I used to be embarrassed wearing swim suits and hot
pants because of discoloration; but after a while, I forgot all about it
and learned to accept it.

My mom used to jokingly blame Aunt Lucille for *burning my
baby*, but she never outwardly told her that. She didn't want to hurt
her feelings. I was always trying to get into people's cups of coffees
my mother told me. It wasn't the first time I had had a cup of coffee.
That's why my mom would say Aunt Lucille did it on purpose 'cause
she was mean and spiteful and knew better than to give me that

119

hot coffee and leave me alone with it, but I played a part in it too. I should have listened, *but I was baby.* I had to walk around with a big old patch on my butt, and I couldn't wear panties, so my mother told me to stay in the house. But I never did. My brother's friends used to laugh at me because I wanted to follow them, and my cousin Charles would always go get his friends and show them my burned booty. So you see why I said even before, I became addicted to crack and lived on the streets. I had already been groomed to show my good and plenty to people? I'm laughing, but I think about these things.

I moved back to Blythe when I was fifteen years old, and I ran into one of my brother's old friends, Cornel Stinson Jr. He was trying to talk to me, and he asked me my name. I told him, "Lena."

He started laughing and said, "Not the little burnt booty girl that used to run around Jackson Court naked?" And he laughed again. And in between his snickering, he coyly asked, "Can I see if it healed?"

We both laughed, and I said, "No, it healed just fine." As I look back over my life, I can see that little story as a sign of how my life would be burned, exposed, and uninhibited; and I would be laughed at. But I thank God for saving me then and saving me later in my life again. He said in Isaiah that we would go through the fire and not get burned (Isaiah 43:2). I know He wasn't talking about getting burned with coffee, but I have come through some fires in my life that a cup of coffee could not even measure up to. I have a soft spot in my heart for burned victims.

When we left Blythe, and we moved to Los Angeles, a friend of mine (Anita Drake) and I were walking along the sidewalk on Twenty-Third and Wall Street near the corner of where we once lived before they store that big house down. I was wearing a Dashiki, an African-like covering that was made out of cotton fabric. It was during the time when the Black Panthers were reuniting black people, and we kids were emulating them with Afros and trying to dress as they did. I was being devilish, playing with matches, as I had a habit of doing and Anita kept telling me to stop striking them; but I wouldn't listen. Anita, who we all called Nidy, was the good girl of us two. I was good too, but I liked getting into stuff and experimenting.

It's a wonder I didn't become a scientist. I was smoking cigarettes, trying to drink, and playing spin the bottle, fighting and hanging with the boys, playing hide and go get it, you name it. I was into it. This was in 1968, and I was ten years old. Nidy was my best friend, and she was my conscious. She was always telling me to be good, or I wasn't going to make it to heaven. I heard her, but I didn't listen.

On this day that I am writing about, I had gone to her house and asked her to walk to the store with me. As we walked along the sidewalk, I was cussing and just being my usual rambunctious self; and every time I cussed, I would ask God to forgive me, and she said, "Lena, God ain't gone keep forgiving you every time you cuss, and you were baptized!"

I answered her with a negative response, something to the tune of so; or I don't care, and yes he would. I kept flicking the matches as we walked. I would flick them from the match book and watch them fly into the air, and Nidy said with authority (she was older than I was), "And you betta' stop playing with the matches!"

But it didn't make a difference because in hindsight, I felt as though my badness overruled her being older than me.

By the time we had gotten to the corner of Wall Street, I flicked a match and I felt a *whoosh* come over me; and my face, heat seem to blow around me, but there was no wind. I dropped the match book and yelled "Whoa!' And Anita and I stopped, and my eyes were big from excitement. I looked at Nidy and said, "I was on fire!"

And Anita looked at me and said, "Stop lying. God gone get you for lying," she added. And I tried to convince her, then I said "Look at my dress!" And sure enough, the spark of the match had popped backwards instead of frontward; and it singed my dress from the neck to the stomach area.

We both looked at each other; and Anita said, nonchalantly, "See, I told you to stop playing with matches." And we walked on to the store, making small talk. Neither of us realizing the depth of that moment.

I didn't have to be told that an Angel of God blew that fire out before it could burn me in any way. This was just another example of how God had me covered in my life, and I just didn't see it or get it. As fast as the fire went *poof* around me, I was into something else.

Wall Street had some nice houses on it, and it had houses that were duplexes and four-plexes on one side. We had moved to some courts that was near Trinity Park. The park was so close, we could climb the fence and still be right in the park; and sometimes, we did that just to be doing something. We stayed on the left side of the courts. It was two apartments on the left and two on the right, with a huge square of cement that served as a porch and the steps to get into the apartment. These were common styles places in LA. I was in the house in broad daylight alone looking for my shoes. My mama was in the back at the bookie joint. There was one big house in the back of the courts where all the grown-ups hung out, drinking, and listening to the horse races. If I had to draw how the places look, it would be like an upside down *u*. My mother had been back there a while, and my daddy was at work, and my brother was gone as well. I had gone to find some matches to strike, to look under the bed for my shoes, and *Poof!* The mattress ignited almost before I could move my face. The smoke began to find its way from under the bed, as though long skeletal fingers were trying to claw their way out. I panicked and ran.

I ran to the *big house* where I knew my mother was; and as I bust into the door, they all jumped. My mom asked in a startled voice, "What the hell wrong with you?" She knew I knew that no kids were allowed in the bookie joint, not even her own unless she had called for us, and usually to run errands or get her something to eat from our house. Then she noticed the paper thin belt I held in my hand, and she asked me, "Girl, what have you done?"

And as I stood crying, I kept saying, "Here, Mama, I know you gone whoop me!" And she kept trying to get me to tell her what had I done.

By then, the neighborhood drunk and handyman named Sammy bust in the door and said, "Doris, you better get your ass up your house on fire!" and she jumped up and pushed me aside and ran out the door. Mr. Jack was renting the house, and he was in charge of the joint, so it was a good thing he had come that day because my mother took off and left everything: money, scratch sheets (for the races), and me. I later heard the sirens, and Mr. Jack and I went to the door to peek, to see what was going on. I still had the flimsy belt in my hand. After I saw the smoke crawling from under the bed, I took the time to go through my mother's closet to *find a belt for her, more like find a belt for me* 'cause I knew where *Big Bertha* was. That was the one she used when she got the belt on her own.

The street was filled with firemen and police officers, and people had come out their houses to see the excitement. I was still in the back house crying and waiting on that whooping that I knew was coming, and it came too! The fireman asked who started the fire, and my mother called me to the front sidewalk, and he started to tell me about the dangers of playing with matches and how this could have been a big disaster, had it not been contained, and how the landlord was going to have to charge my parents for the damage and how I could go to jail for starting a fire like that. I was standing there listening to that man, but all I was thinking about was my mama whooping my tail. After the police and the fireman said it was safe to go in the house, my mama grabbed my hand and marched me up the big cement porch and went into the closet and reached for the Big Bertha belt; and it wasn't there. She turned around to look at me and said, "You bettah find that dam belt, and find it now!"

I had thrown it behind the couch in the front room before I had gone to tell her about the fire; and as soon as I handed it to her, she tore my butt up.

I was called firebug by the kids, knowing they had heard it from the grown-ups, that's how their kids knew to say it. The only difference was that I couldn't say much to the older folks, but I beat up the kids who messed with me or tried to if I could catch them from running. I know that as I look back and reminisce about the childhood I lived, I can see the hand of God on me, covering me and all around me. He had been with me in some of my smallest moments to some of the great events that followed in my life. He has brought me through many more fires than the one on Wall Street that day. Fires that had no flames but were the trials and tribulations that I had to face growing up. He brought me through sexual abuse, drug addiction, homelessness, depression; and I could go on. But more than anything, He brought me through it all, learning it was time to stop protecting everyone because no one had been protecting me. My mother's death was a fire for me, but I am making it through that realization as well. I have triumphed unharmed, being refined and being blessed still. After forty something years—and I am not bragging nor glorifying the life I lived—I am celebrating Jesus, that through all my fires, I can still look in the mirror and see the face of one very mischievous and vigorous child; and praise God for the fires that has lead me to the arms of Christ.

Revelation 3:18 states, "And I counsel thee to buy of me gold tried in the fire, that thou mayest be rich; and white raiment, that thou mayest be clothed and that the shame of thy nakedness do not appear and anoint thine eyes with eye salve that thou mayest see."

This scripture touches my heart, and I believe that God is refining me daily. I don't know all that God has planned for me, but I know that He has walked beside me on many sidewalks of my life. He kept me safe from harm along the way; and as I travel down many more sidewalks in my life finding new *sidewalk tales* to share, I will definitely know now that I never walk alone.

About the Author

Photo credit: Joseph Damani McDole

Arlene Rogers Wilhite was born in the small town of Blythe, California, the last town on California's Interstate—10 eastbound. It was once a thriving agricultural town that is now a town of dusty hopes and dreams of many that she loves and hopes to one day retire to, to continue her love of writing and serving her community. She was in a doctoral program at the time of this writing and striving to successfully complete that arduous journey with the goals of helping to rebuild hopes and dreams of children and individuals in her hometown of Blythe, California. She is the mother of three adult children and twelve grandchildren with a hosts of god-grandchildren, nieces, and nephews that she loves and lives for.

Sidewalk Tales is her first completed book that is very dear to her, as it was a therapeutic journey that helped her to face her childhood sexual abuse, her alcohol and drug addictions, incarceration, her bullying and being a bully, and her fears of believing that she was worthless and had no future because she thought she was tainted; and no one would love or respect her.

Arlene began writing, over-achieving, and overly compensating, and placing herself in dangerous situations to survive; but deep within her, she knew there was a real loving and kind person within her that was trying to step out of the shell of a person, hardships tried to make her out to be. On that journey—the journey that lead to 'her' and finding out who she was—she accomplished a GED, two *AAs*, one BA, two master's degree, and many honors and awards for community work that she now uses for examples to tell others that she knows now had it not been for God in her life, love for herself, and much determination, she would never have released the pain and joy and growth she found in each story of *Sidewalk Tales*. *DVD-Testimony available through author (928) 216-9243

CPSIA information can be obtained
at www.ICGtesting.com
Printed in the USA
BVHW040202110323
660181BV00007B/638

9 781684 560103